D1450429

The Big Book
of Sex Quotes

The Big Book of Sex Quotes

Compiled by
Julian L'Estrange

CASSELL

Weidenfeld & Nicolson
Wellington House, 125 Strand, London WC2R 0BB

First published 2004

© Compilation copyright Weidenfeld & Nicolson

All rights reserved. No part of this publication may be
reproduced or transmitted in any form or by any means,
electronic or mechanical including photocopying,
recording or any information storage or retrieval system,
without prior permission in writing from the publishers
and copyright owners.

A CIP record for this book is available from the British
Library.

ISBN 0-304-36679-X
Design by www.carrstudio.co.uk
Printed and bound in Great Britain by Clays Ltd,
St Ives plc

www.orionbooks.co.uk

Contents

Introduction

When those smut-mongers at Weidenfeld & Nicolson approached me to compile what they were pleased to call *The Big Book of Sex Quotes* I was, as you may imagine, somewhat taken aback. Indeed, I was at considerable pains to conceal the letter from Mrs L'Estrange, who has strong views on these matters and has been known to snip out the more alluring photographs of starlets from the *Telegraph* newspaper prior to its appearance alongside the kippers at breakfast.

Although I am known in certain circles for such specialized works as 'Making the Sparks Fly: Frottage in the Era of Synthetic Fabrics' (*Proceedings of the International Conference on Textile Technology*, Cambridge, 1987), something as *popular* as the volume proposed by Messrs W. & N. was, I argued in reply, hardly my cup of tea. However, when a large package arrived by courier replete with bundles of used fivers, I felt there was no alternative but to comply with their importunate desires.

'Just you make sure you get loadsa celebs in there, Jules old son,' said one's editor, ever the populist. 'Plenty soap slags is wot the punters want, right? Three-in-a-bed romps, I woz Prince Chaz's dildo 'n' such, not fuckin Ovid and wosname Catullus. And keep off the old Bard, wontcha? Though I reckon we could always slip the Swan of Avon in under Bestiality, arf arf arf.'

I held my tongue.

The business of compiling this modest tome has, I must confess, been something of an education. We learn, for example, that, according to the Chinese sage Sun-szu-mo, to refrain from ejaculation leads to ulcers and boils; that the G-spot is in fact in the ear (although why in this case Mrs L'Estrange should have demanded I withdraw my tongue therefrom is a mystery); that the FBI are powerless to act in cases of oral-genital intimacy, unless it has in some way obstructed interstate commerce; that 82 per cent of British men would prefer to sleep with a goat than the Duchess of York; that Miss Halle Berry enjoyed a *ménage à trois* with her partner and a certain Oscar; that Mr Richard Gere has confessed himself a lesbian; that Madonna (apparently one of those 'tabloid totties' one's editor is so partial to) would rather read a book; and that the chicken did indeed come before the egg.

The whole experience has, needless to say, been a bit much for a man of my age and condition, it having been many a year since Mrs L'Estrange was persuaded to drop her tweeds and think of England. However, I console myself with the words of a sermon at Oxford recalled by T.E. Lawrence (a.k.a. Lawrence of Arabia) in the early years of the last century:

Let me implore you, my young friends, not to imperil your immortal souls upon a pleasure which, so I am credibly informed, lasts less than one and three-quarter minutes.

Amen to that, say I.

JULIAN L'ESTRANGE
Dungettinany
Waterloo Road
Stoke Newington

In Praise of **SEX** (Mostly)

Sex is part of nature. I go along with nature.

Marilyn Monroe

To err is human – but it feels divine.

Mae West

Sex is like money. Only too much is enough.

John Updike, Couples *(1968)*

I'd like to meet the person who invented sex and see what they're working on now.

Anon.

Sex is the most fun I have ever had without laughing.

Woody Allen, Annie Hall *(1977)*

I read so many bad things about sex I had to give up reading.

Anon.

Sex is the short cut to everything.

Anne Cumming, The Love Quest *(1991)*

Sex got me into trouble from the age of fifteen:
I'm hoping that by the time I'm seventy I'll
straighten it out.
Harold Robbins

Sex is bad for one.
But it's good for two.
T-shirt slogan, 1970s

At certain times I like sex – like after a cigarette.
Rodney Dangerfield

The sex was so good that even the neighbours
had a cigarette.
Anon.

WHAT THE GOOD BOOK SAYS   1

BE FRUITFUL AND MULTIPLY, AND FILL THE WATERS IN
THE SEAS, AND LET FOWL MULTIPLY IN THE EARTH.
GENESIS 1:22

And yet:

OF THE DELIGHTS OF THIS WORLD MAN CARES MOST
FOR SEXUAL INTERCOURSE, YET HE HAS LEFT IT OUT OF
HIS HEAVEN.
MARK TWAIN

*The wren goes to't, and the small gilded fly
Does lecher in my sight.
Let copulation thrive!*

William Shakespeare, *King Lear, IV.vi*

*Life can little more supply
Than just a few good fucks and then we die.*

John Wilkes and Thomas Potter,
An Essay on Woman (1763)

*Gin a body meet a body
Comin' thro' the rye;
Gin a body fuck a body,
Need a body cry?*

Robert Burns (unbowdlerized)

Sex is not the answer. Sex is the question. 'Yes' is the answer.

Swami X

Sex is one of the nine reasons for reincarnation; the other eight are unimportant.

Henry Miller, Big Sur and the Oranges of Hieronymus Bosch *(1958)*

It doesn't matter what you do in the bedroom as long as you don't do it in the street and frighten the horses.

Mrs Patrick Campbell

Of all sexual aberrations, chastity is the strangest.

Jacques Anatole Thibault

There may be some things better than sex and some things may be worse, but there is nothing exactly like it.

W.C. Fields

Sexual intercourse is kicking death in the ass while singing.

Charles Bukowski

'Bed', as the Italian proverb succinctly puts it, 'is the poor man's opera.'

Aldous Huxley, Heaven and Hell *(1956)*

I love sex. It's free and doesn't require special shoes.

Anon.

I think sex is better than logic, but I can't prove it.

Graffito

WORDS FROM THE WISE

A Doctor writes:

Sexual love is undoubtedly one of the chief things in life ... Apart from a few queer fanatics, all the world knows this ...

Sigmund Freud, Observations on Transference-Love *(1915)*

A Physicist writes:

Science is a lot like sex. Sometimes something useful comes of it, but that's not the reason we're doing it.

Richard Feynman

A Complete and Utter Pervert writes:

Sex is as important as eating or drinking and we ought to allow the one appetite to be satisfied with as little restraint or false modesty as the other.

Marquis de Sade, L'Histoire de Juliette *(1797)*

Sex **HATERS**

Sex is the biggest nothing of all time.

Andy Warhol

Sex is God's joke on human beings.

Bette Davis

Sex is a bad thing because it rumples the clothes.

Jackie Onassis

Before we make love my husband takes a pain killer.

Joan Rivers

I'd rather have a cup of tea any day.

Boy George

Two minutes of gooey near-satisfaction followed by weeks of haunting guilt is so much more easily attained with Häagen-Dazs.

Florence Campbell

An intellectual is a person who has discovered something more interesting than sex.

Aldous Huxley

Sex is interesting, but it's not totally important.
I mean it's not even as important (physically) as
excretion. A man can go seventy years without
a piece of ass, but he can die in a week without
a bowel movement.

Charles Bukowski, Notes on a Dirty Old Man

The pleasure is momentary, the position
ridiculous, and the expense damnable.

Lord Chesterfield, attributed (18th century)

**I know it does make people
happy but to me it's just
like having a cup of tea.**

Cynthia Payne, brothel-keeper, 8 November 1987

Christianity has done a great
deal for love by making a sin of it.

Anatole France, Le Jardin d'Épicure

Life in Lubbock, Texas, taught me two things: One
is that God loves you and you're going to burn in
hell. The other is that sex is the most awful, filthy
thing on earth and you should save it for someone
you love.

Butch Hancock

Why should we take advice on sex from the pope?
If he knows anything about it, he shouldn't.

George Bernard Shaw

To hear many religious people talk, one would
think God created the torso, head, legs and arms,
but the devil slapped on the genitals.

Don Schrader

Surely the sex business isn't worth all this damned
fuss? I've met only a handful of people who cared
a biscuit for it.

T.E. Lawrence (Lawrence of Arabia), on reading D.H. Lawrence's
Lady Chatterley's Lover

It's all this cold-hearted fucking that is death and
idiocy.

D.H. Lawrence, Lady Chatterley's Lover *(1928)*

Except for the two people who are indulging in it
the sexual act is a comic operation.

Sir Compton Mackenzie, My Life and Times

When authorities warn you of the sinfulness of sex,
there is an important lesson to be learned. Do not
have sex with the authorities.

Matt Groening, 'Basic Sex Facts For Today's Youngfolk', from Life
In Hell

IT IS GOOD FOR A MAN NOT TO TOUCH A WOMAN.
ST PAUL, I CORINTHIANS, 7:1

Paul went on in the same vein:

IT IS BETTER TO MARRY THAN TO BURN.
I CORINTHIANS, 7:9

... and on:

TO BE CARNALLY MINDED IS DEATH.
ROMANS 8:6

Augustine of Hippo continued the cheery theme:

INTER FAECES ET URINAM NASCIMUR.
(Between shit and urine we are born.)
ST AUGUSTINE OF HIPPO, *CONFESSIONS* (4TH CENTURY).
Derek Jarman, in *At Your Own Risk: A Saint's Testament*
(1992), wrote 'Augustine of Hippo ... murdered his way to
sainthood spouting on about the sins located in his genitals.'

An Old Bore writes:

THE ORGASM HAS REPLACED THE CROSS AS THE FOCUS
OF LONGING AND THE IMAGE OF FULFILMENT.
MALCOLM MUGGERIDGE, *TREAD SOFTLY FOR YOU
TREAD ON MY JOKES* (1966)

Once a year I lash my own partner to the kitchen table and wrap him in clingfilm. The purpose of this is not, however, sexual, but rather the only way I can stop him attempting to force his hideously empurpled member into my mouth as I perform my annual wifely duty (on his birthday) by bringing him to a shattering climax using a pair of plastic pasta tongs. The clingfilm is to protect the table, since male ejaculate has a disastrous effect on French polish.

Rowena Raunchbitch, 'Torrid Sex Tips for Red-Hot Lovers', in the Rockall Times, *22 July 2002*

All this fuss about sleeping together. For physical pleasure I'd sooner go to my dentist any day.

Evelyn Waugh, Vile Bodies *(1930)*

Mrs Swabb: Me, I don't bother with sex. I leave that to the experts.

Alan Bennett, Habeas Corpus *(1973)*

Don't have sex, man. It leads to kissing and pretty soon you have to start talking to them.

Steve Martin

LIE BACK AND THINK OF ENGLAND

I am happy now that Charles calls on my bedchamber less frequently than of old. As it is, I now endure but two calls a week and when I hear his steps outside my door I lie down on my bed, close my eyes, open my legs and think of England.

Lady Alice Hillingdon, Journal, *1912*

Contrary to popular belief, English women do not wear tweed nightgowns.

Hermione Gingold, in Saturday Review, *1955*

My mother used to say, Delia, if S-E-X ever rears its ugly head, close your eyes before you see the rest of it.

Alan Ayckbourn, Bedroom Farce *(1978)*

I believe in making the world safe for our children, but not our children's children, because I don't think children should be having sex.

Jack Handey, on Saturday Night Live

SAD OLD MASTERS

Painting and fucking a lot are not compatible; it weakens the brain.

Vincent Van Gogh, letter, June 1888

The art of procreation and the members employed therein are so repulsive, that if it were not for the beauty of the faces and the adornments of the actors and the pent-up impulse, nature would lose the human species.

Leonardo da Vinci

Compare and contrast with:

While Titian was grinding rose madder
His model was posed on a ladder.
Her position to Titian
Suggested coition
So he dashed up the ladder and had her.

Anon.

Misery and Revulsion: Some Grumpy Old Men

Down from the waist they are Centaurs,
Though women all above:
But to the girdle do the gods inherit,
Beneath is all the fiends':
There's hell, there's darkness, there's the sulphurous pit,
Burning, scalding, stench, consumption; fie, fie, fie!

Lear, in William Shakespeare's, *King Lear* (1605)

A man has missed something if he has never woken up in an anonymous bed beside a face he'll never see again, and if he has never left a brothel at dawn, feeling like jumping off a bridge into the river out of sheer physical disgust with life.

Gustave Flaubert

Love causes more pain than pleasure. Pleasure is only illusory. Reason would command us to avoid love, if it were not for the fatal sexual impulse – therefore it would be best to be castrated.

Karl von Hartmann, Philosophie des Unbevursten *(1869)*

After the 'change of life' with women, sexual congress, while permissible, should be infrequent, no less for her sake than that of her husband, whose advancing years should warn him of the medical maxim: 'Each time a man delivers himself to this indulgence, he casts a shovelful of earth upon his coffin.'

Nicholas Francis Croke, Satan in Society *(1876)*

The sexual parts are not only vivid examples of the body's dominion; they are also apertures whose damp emissions and ammoniac smells testify to the mysterious putrefaction of the body.

Roger Scruton, Sexual Desire *(1986)*

I could be content that we might procreate like trees, without conjunction, or that there were any way to perpetuate the World without this trivial and vulgar way of coition: it is the foolishest act a wise man commits in all his life …

Sir Thomas Browne, *Religio Medici* (1643)

Nothing in our culture, not even home computers, is more overrated than the epidermal felicity of two featherless bipeds in desperate congress.

Quentin Crisp

Giving the Judge an **ERECTION**

Obscenity and Censorship

See also Pornucopia.

Obscenity is whatever gives the judge an erection.

Anon.

It's hard to be funny when you have to be clean.

Mae West

You can prick your finger, but you can't finger your prick.

George Carlin

Obscenity can be found in any book except the telephone directory.

George Bernard Shaw

Of Henry Miller's *Tropic of Cancer* (1934):

At last, an unprintable book that is readable.

Ezra Pound

We have long passed the Victorian era, when asterisks were followed after a certain interval by a baby.

W. Somerset Maugham, The Constant Wife *(1926)*

On film censorship in the 1950s and early 1960s:

In love scenes on beds you had to keep one foot on the floor at all times, which made it rather like snooker or pool. If you lifted that one foot off the floor, it was a foul shot.

Albert Finney

They are doing things on the screen these days that the French don't even put on postcards.

Bob Hope, in 1970

I always found it a good policy to slip a few items into a script that the censors would cut out. It gave them a sense of accomplishing their job and they were less likely to cut out the things I really wanted to keep in.

Mae West, Goodness Had Nothing To Do With It *(1959)*

Would you allow your wife or your servant to read this book?

Mervyn Griffith-Jones, prosecuting counsel in the Crown vs Penguin Books, 1960, in the matter of D.H. Lawrence's Lady Chatterley's Lover

Murder is a crime.
Describing murder is not.
Sex is not a crime. Describing sex is.

Gershon Legman

Sexual intercourse began
In nineteen sixty-three
(Which was rather late for
me) –
Between the end of the
Chatterley ban
And the Beatles' first LP.

*Philip Larkin, 'Annus Mirabilis'
(1974)*

Oh *That's* What
IT'S FOR

Reproduction

Familiarity breeds contempt – and children.

Mark Twain, Notebooks

Love is only a dirty trick played on us to assure the continuation of the species.

W. Somerset Maugham, A Writer's Notebook *(1949)*

The orgasm is the sugar coating with which the Creator (or Nature) has disguised the bitter pill of reproduction.

Paul A. Robinson, The Sexual Radicals *(1953)*

It is not economical to go to bed early to save the candles if the result is twins.

Chinese proverb

My wife just got pregnant – she took seriously what was poked at her in fun.

Anon.

MARRIAGE FILLS THE EARTH, VIRGINITY HEAVEN.
ST JEROME, ADVERSUS IOVINIANUM (4TH CENTURY)

No matter how much cats fight, there always seem to be plenty of kittens.
Abraham Lincoln

This 'relationship' business is one big waste of time. It is just Mother Nature urging you to breed, breed, breed. Learn from nature. Learn from our friend the spider. Just mate once and then kill him.
Ruby Wax

Literature is mostly about sex and not much about having children and life is the other way round.
David Lodge, The British Museum is Falling Down *(1965)*

The reproduction of mankind is a great marvel and mystery. Had God consulted me in the matter, I should have advised him to continue the generation of the species by fashioning them out of clay.
Martin Luther

To a contestant on his quiz show who had had 22 children, explaining 'I love my husband':

I like my cigar too, but I take it out once in a while.
Groucho Marx, quoted in Dorothy Herrman, With Malice Toward All *(1982)*

Let's fuck, dear heart, let's have it in and out,
For we're obliged to fuck for being born,
And as I crave for cunt, you ache for horn,
Because the world would not make sense without.

Pietro Aretino, 'Let's Fuck, Dear Heart'
(16th century)

For once you must try not to shirk the facts:
Mankind is kept alive by bestial acts.

Bertolt Brecht, *The Threepenny Opera* (1929)

Are we not brutes to call the act that makes us,
'brutish'?

Michel de Montaigne, 'On Virgil' (16th century)

I pour the stuff to start sons and daughters fit for
these States, I press with slow rude muscle,
I brace myself effectually, I listen to no entreaties,
I dare not withdraw till I deposit what has so long
accumulated within me.

Walt Whitman, 'Children of Adam' (1860)

The most common form of marriage proposal: 'You're what?!?'

Anon.

We all worry about the population explosion, but we don't worry about it at the right time.

Arthur Hoppe

When a brigadier in the Indian Army asked his married manservant of many years why he had no children, the latter replied:

Ah, my wife, sir – she's inconceivable and impregnable.

College is like a woman: you work so hard to get in, and nine months later you wish you'd never come.

Anon.

One for the conspiracy theorists. Italy is seriously concerned about its declining birth rate. And then the whole of mainland Italy is plunged into a prolonged blackout.

Stanley Alderson, letter to the Guardian, *1 October 2003, referring to the power cut that affected 57 million Italians*

When we were trying to conceive, I would douse my balls in icy cold water before intercourse.

Richard Madeley (that's Richard as in Judy)

Oh what a tangled web we weave when first we practise to conceive.

Don Herold

There was a lady who triplets begat
Nat, Pat and Tat
It was fun breeding
But trouble feeding
Cause she didn't have a tit for Tat.

Anon.

INFERTILITY UNLIKELY TO BE PASSED ON

Headline from the Montgomery Advertiser

STUDY FINDS SEX–PREGNANCY LINK

Headline from the Cornell Daily Sun, *7 December 1995*

TEENAGE GIRLS OFTEN HAVE BABIES FATHERED BY MEN

Headline from the Sunday Oregonian

Abstinence (But Not Yet)

See also Deprived of Depravity: Not Getting Any.

DA MIHI CASTITATEM ET CONTINENTEM, SED NOLI
MODO.
(Give me chastity and continence, but not yet.)
ST AUGUSTINE, CONFESSIONS

We may eventually come to realize that chastity is
no more a virtue than malnutrition.
Alex Comfort

I consider sex a misdemeanour, the more I miss,
de meaner I get.
Mae West

Fastidiousness is the ability to resist a temptation
in the hope that a better one will come along.
Oscar Wilde

Abstainer. *n.* A weak person who yields to the
temptation of denying himself a pleasure.
Ambrose Bierce, The Devil's Dictionary *(1911)*

MEDICAL CONSEQUENCES OF ABSTINENCE

It is a bad thing for a man to go for too long without ejaculating semen for then he will find himself a prey to ulcers and boils.

Sun-szu-mo (7th century)

I wonder how it is with you, Harold? If I don't have a woman for three days, I get a terrible headache.

President J.F. Kennedy, remark to Harold Macmillan, quoted in Alastair Horne, Macmillan 1957–1986 *(1989)*

That melancholy sexual perversion known as continence.

Aldous Huxley, Antic Hay *(1923)*

Virginity can be lost by a thought.

St Jerome

There was a young lady called Wylde,
Who kept herself quite undefiled
By thinking of Jesus,
Contagious diseases
And the bother of having a child.

Norman Douglas, limerick (1917)

To the actor-manager David Garrick:

I'll come no more behind your scenes, David; for the silk stockings and white bosoms of your actresses excite my amorous propensities.

Samuel Johnson

I'm what nature abhors – an old maid. A frozen asset.

The Women *(1939), screenplay by Anita Loos and Jane Murfin, after a play by Clare Booth Luce*

If you resolve to give up smoking, drinking and loving, you don't actually live longer; it just seems longer.

Clement Freud, quoted in the Observer, *27 December 1964*

It is one of the superstitions of the human mind to have imagined that virginity could be a virtue.

Voltaire

A Vision in Pink writes:

I'll wager you that in ten years it will be fashionable again to be a virgin.

Barbara Cartland, in the 1970s

On sex scandals in the era of AIDS:

The more you don't do it, the more it's fun to read about.

Caryl Churchill, Serious Money *(1987)*

Get Yer
YA-YAS OUT
Modesty and Immodesty

The Dean undressed
With heaving breast,
The bishop's wife to lie on.
He thought it lewd
To do it nude,
So he kept his old school tie on.

Anon.

Tiffany: I'll finish dressing.
Bond: Oh please don't. Not on my account.

Lines from the film Diamonds are Forever *(1971)*

When I was young it was considered immodest
for the bride to do anything on the honeymoon
except to weep gently and ask for glasses of
water.

Noël Coward

One Victorian bridegroom, with admirable sensitivity, is said to have left the nuptial chamber to allow his blushing new wife to get ready for bed. After a suitable interval he returned. His heart leaped for joy, for there she lay, stretched out on the silken sheets, the object of all his desires. Unable to restrain himself any longer, he flung himself eagerly on the four-poster. But the bride did not stir. In fact she was out cold, drugged to the tip of her toes. Pinned to the pillow was this note, 'Mummy says you should do what you wish.'

Simon Welfare, Great Honeymoon Disasters *(1986)*

It's not that I'm prudish. It's just that my mother told me never to enter any man's room in months ending in 'R'.

Irene Dunne to Charles Boyer, in the film Love Affair *(1939)*

There was a young person of Tottenham
Whose manners, Good Lord! She'd forgotten 'em.
When she went to the vicar's,
She took off her knickers,
Because she said she was hot in 'em.

Anon.

There was a young girl of Shanghai
Who was so exceedingly shy,
That undressing at night
She turned out the light
For fear of the all-seeing eye.

Bertrand Russell

I'm an intensely shy and vulnerable woman. My
husband has never seen me naked. Nor has he
expressed the least desire to do so.

Dame Edna Everage (aka Barry Humphries), Housewife Superstar
(1976)

Whenever my teenage daughter comes down the
stairs dressed like a tramp for her date, I think to
myself: 'Damn, why won't her mother wear
something like that?'

Dave Henry

There was a young girl of Odessa –
A rather unblushing transgressor.
When sent to the priest
The lewd little beast
Began to undress her confessor.

Anon.

Adam and **EVE**

In the Garden of Eden lay Adam,
Complacently stroking his Madam.
And loud was his mirth
For he knew that on Earth
There were only two balls and he had 'em.

Anon.

Adam and Eve had an ideal marriage. He didn't
have to hear about all the men she could have
married, and she didn't have to hear about the
way his mother cooked.

Anon.

When Eve said to Adam
'Start calling me Madam'
The world became far more exciting;
Which turns to confusion
The modern delusion
That sex is a question of lighting.

Noël Coward

If Adam had had a real hairy back, we probably wouldn't be here today.

Dave Henry

If homosexuality were normal, God would have created Adam and Bruce.

Anita Bryant, US anti-gay campaigner

One day, God calls on Adam and says, 'Adam, I have some good news and some bad news. The good news is that I gave you a penis and a brain. The bad news is that I only gave you enough blood to operate one organ at a time.'

Anon.

Nothing but Sex
MISSPELLED

Love vs Sex

Love ain't nothing but sex misspelled.

Harlan Ellison

Love is friendship plus sex.

Havelock Ellis

The only difference between friends and lovers is about four minutes.

Scott Roeben

Sex without love is merely healthy exercise.

Robert Heinlein

Sex relieves tension – love causes it.

Woody Allen

If love is the answer could you rephrase the question?

Lily Tomlin

I think I could fall madly in bed with you.

Anon.

Q: Do you love me?
A: What do you think? That I'm doing push-ups?

Anon.

What is commonly called love, namely the desire of satisfying a voracious appetite with a certain quantity of delicate white human flesh.

Henry Fielding, *Tom Jones* (1749)

Love is the delightful interval between meeting a beautiful girl and discovering that she looks like a haddock.

John Barrymore

Lisa: Wot's it feel like bein' in love, Kytie?
Katie: Ow, it's prime, Liza. It's like 'avin 'ot treacle runnin' daown yer back!

Caption to Punch *cartoon, 25 January 1899*

Love is the word used to label the sexual excitement of the young, the habituation of the middle-aged and the mutual dependence of the old.

John Ciardi

Sex concentrates on what is on the outside of the individual. It's funny because I think it's better on the inside.

Alex Walsh

Love is not the dying moan of a distant violin – it's the triumphant twang of a bedspring.

S.J. Perelman

Everybody I know has a different idea of love. One girl I know said, 'I knew he loved me when he didn't come in my mouth.'

Andy Warhol, From A to B and Back Again *(1975)*

Sex, on the whole, was meant to be short, nasty and brutish. If what you want is cuddling, you should buy a puppy.

Julie Burchill, Sex and Sensibility *(1992)*

Nothing makes you forget about love like sex.

Staci Beasley

Now the whole dizzying and delirious range of sexual possibilities has been boiled down to that one big, boring, bulimic word, RELATIONSHIP.

Julie Burchill, Sex and Sensibility *(1992)*

Love is the answer – but while you're waiting for the answer sex raises some pretty good questions.

Woody Allen

For me, love is very deep, but sex only has to go a few inches.

Stacy Nelkin

Anybody who believes that the way to a man's heart is through his stomach flunked geography.

Robert Byrne

The big mistake that men make is that when they turn 13 or 14 all of a sudden they believe they like women. Actually, they're just horny.

Jules Feiffer

Sex without love is an empty experience, but as empty experiences go it's one of the best.

Woody Allen

Love is a matter of chemistry, but sex is a matter of physics.

Anon.

Love is being able to squeeze your lover's spots.

Zoe Ball

Carrying **ON**

Tony (disguised as hotel detective): Have you got a woman in there?
Hackenbush: If I haven't, I've wasted thirty minutes of valuable time.

Lines from A Day at the Races *(1937)*

Happiness is watching the TV at your girlfriend's house during a power failure.

Bob Hope

There was an old maid of Pitlochry
Whose morals were truly a mockery,
For under her bed
Was a lover instead
Of the usual porcelain crockery.

Anon.

Hooray, hooray, the first of May,
Outdoor fucking begins today.

Graffito

There is nothing wrong with making love with the light on. Just make sure the car door is closed.

George Burns

My own belief is that there is hardly anyone whose sexual life, if it were broadcast, would not fill the world at large with surprise and horror.

W. Somerset Maugham

Poets' Corner 3

Out upon it, I have lov'd
Three whole days together;
And am like to love three more,
If it prove fair weather.

John Suckling, 'A Poem with the Answer' (1659)

A little still she strove, and much repented,
And whispering 'I will ne'er consent' – consented.

Lord Byron, *Don Juan* (1819–24)

He in a few minutes ravished this fair creature, or at
least would have ravished her, if she had not, by a
timely compliance, prevented him.

Henry Fielding, *Jonathan Wild* (1743)

Called to see you but you were in.

Karl Miller, note left on the door of a fellow undergraduate whom
he had found entertaining a young lady

College warden: Are you entertaining a woman in your room?
Student: I'll just ask her.

Anon.

I like my sex the way I play basketball: one on one with as little dribbling as possible.

Leslie Nielsen

Limericks

The limerick packs laughs anatomical
Into space that is quite economical.
But the good ones I've seen
So seldom are clean
And the clean ones seldom are comical.

Anon.

The limerick's an art-form complex
Whose contents run chiefly to sex.
It's famous for virgins
And masculine urgin's
And vulgar erotic effects.

Anon.

My girlfriend told me I should be more affec-
tionate. So I got two girlfriends.

Anon.

Q: Does your wife smoke after sexual intercourse?
A: I don't know, I've never looked.

Anon.

Green with lust and sick with sickness,
Let me lick your lacquered toes.
Gosh, O Gosh your Royal Highness
Put your finger up my nose.

The eccentric Oxford academic Maurice Bowra's paean to
Princess Margaret, in the style of John Betjeman.
Quoted in the Guardian, *11 February 2002*

Sex APPEAL

Sex appeal is fifty per cent what you've got and fifty per cent what people think you've got.

Sophia Loren

I believe it's better to be looked over than it is to be overlooked.

Mae West, Belle of the Nineties *(1934)*

Being a sex symbol has to do with an attitude, not looks. Most men think it's looks, most women know otherwise.

Kathleen Turner, quoted in the Observer, *27 April, 1986*

I don't try to be a sex bomb. I am one.

Kylie Minogue

Men seldom make passes
At girls who wear glasses.

Dorothy Parker, 'News Item'

When she raises her eyelids it's as if she were taking off all her clothes.

Colette, Claudine and Annie *(1903)*

Millihelen. *n.* the amount of beauty required to launch one ship.

Anon.

There was a young lassie from Morton,
Who had one long tit and one short 'un,
On top of all that,
A great hairy twat,
And a fart like a six-fifty Norton.

Anon.

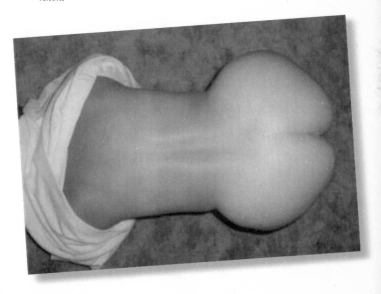

Lingerie and **LESS**

The greatest provocations of lust are from the apparel.
Robert Burton, *Anatomy of Melancholy* (1621)

Brevity is the soul of lingerie – as the Petticoat said to the Chemise.
Dorothy Parker, apparently a caption to an illustration in Vogue *in 1916*

A lady is one who never shows her underwear unintentionally.
Lillian Day, Kiss and Tell *(1931)*

Underwear is such an emotional thing.
Elle 'While My G-String Gently Weeps' MacPherson

The drawers of a spinster from Lavenham
Had rude limericks embroidered in Slav on 'em.
To her lawyer she said,
'Burn them all when I'm dead,
For I'm damned if my nephew is havin' 'em.'
Anon.

A bikini is like a barbed-wire fence. It protects the property without obstructing the view.
Joey Adams

I'm into cotton underwear. I don't need cheetah-print leather to make me feel sexy.

Nelly Furtado

I've just bought myself a G-string –
which is rather fun.

Laurence Llewelyn-Bowen

It wouldn't be a good idea
To let him stay.
When they knew each other better –
Not today.
But she put on her new black knickers
Anyway.

Wendy Cope, 'Prelude'

*Mahoney (when asked if she is in mourning for her
lately demised boyfriend): I'm wearing black
underwear.*

Film version of Dick Tracey *(1990)*

A lady removing her scanties
Heard them crackle electrical chanties.
Said her husband, 'My dear,
I very much fear
You suffer from amps in your panties.'

Anon.

STORM IN A D-CUP: BRAS AND BUSTS

Definition of a Stone Age bra:

An over-shoulder boulder-holder.

Anon.

Q: What did the brassière say to the top hat?
A: You go on ahead while I give these two a lift.

Related by Freya Stark to the British ambassador in Cairo in 1942, much to the latter's shock

What an effective bra should do:

Round 'em up and head 'em out.

Anon.

Q: Do you know why they call it the Wonderbra?
A: When you take it off you wonder where the tits went.

Anon.

Husband: I don't know why you wear a bra, you've got nothing to put in it.
Wife: You wear briefs, don't you?

Anon.

Seamed stockings aren't subtle but they certainly do the job. You shouldn't wear them when out with someone you're not prepared to sleep with, since their presence is tantamount to saying, 'Hi there, big fellow, please rip my clothes off at your earliest opportunity.' If you really want your escort paralytic with lust, stop frequently to adjust the seams.

Cynthia Heimel, Sex Tips for Girls *(1983)*

I think the only good thing to be said about leotards is that they're a very effective deterrent against any sort of unwanted sexual attention. If you're wearing stretch knickers, and stretch tights, and a stretch Lycra leotard, you might as well try and sexually harass a trampoline.

Victoria Wood

Nude, Bare-Arsed and Stark-Bollock
NAKED

If God had wanted us to walk around naked, we would have been born that way.

Anon.

A nudist resort in Benares
Took a midget in all unawares.
But he made members weep
For he just couldn't keep
His nose out of private affairs.

Anon.

What a man enjoys about a woman's clothes are his fantasies of how she would look without them.

Brendan Francis

The trouble with nude dancing is that not everything stops when the music stops.

Robert Helpmann

You wear a nightgown, robe and girdle, even in
* hot weather;*
I like sleeping with a woman in the altogether.

Martial, *Epigrams* (1st century AD)

No beauty doth she miss
When all her robes are on:
But Beauty's self she is
When all her robes are gone.

Anon. madrigal (17th century)

There once was a lady of Erskine
Who had remarkably fair skin.
When I said to her, 'Mabel,
You look well in sable,'
She replied, 'I look best in my bearskin.'
Anon.

I didn't pay three pounds fifty just to see half a
dozen acorns and a chipolata.

Noël Coward, referring to the male nude scenes in David Storey's
play The Changing Room *(1972)*

AND THEY WERE BOTH NAKED, THE MAN AND HIS WIFE,
AND WERE NOT ASHAMED.
GENESIS 2:25

There once was a sculptor called Phidias
Who had a distaste for the hideous.
So he sculpt Aphrodite
Without any nightie
Which shocked the ultra-fastidious.

Anon.

A One-Balled Nazi writes:

The total exposure of the human body is
undignified as well as an error of taste.

Adolf Hitler

Captain Cock,
Brigadier Balls and
PRIVATE PARTS

See also Erections and Other Feats of Engineering.

The penis is mightier than the sword.

Mark Twain

The brain is viewed as an appendage of the genital glands.

Carl Jung

My brain is my second favourite organ.

Woody Allen, Sleeper *(1973)*

There once was a big man from Ghent
Who had a penis so long that it bent;
It was so much trouble
That he kept it bent double
And instead of coming he went.

Anon.

Men read maps better because only a male mind could conceive of an inch equalling a hundred miles.

Roseanne Barr

There is one important thing about penises all girls should know: penises really do have different sizes. From smallest to largest:
– Small
– Medium
– Oh, God ...
– Does that come in white?

Anon.

There once was a young man called Stencil
Whose prick was as sharp as a pencil.
He punctured an actress,
Two sheets and a mattress,
And dented the bedroom utensil.

Anon.

When others kid me about being bald, I simply tell them that the way I figure it, the good Lord only gave men so many hormones, and if others want to waste theirs on growing hair, that's up to them.

John Glenn, astronaut and US senator

Life is like a penis: when it's soft you can't beat it, and when it's hard you get fucked.

Anon.

There was a young fellow named Kimble
Whose penis was exceedingly nimble,
But fragile and slender,
And dainty and tender,
So he kept it encased in a thimble.

Anon.

'How tall are you?'
'Six foot seven.'
'Let's forget about the six feet and talk about the seven inches.'

Mae West

Lady, if I were built in proportion, I'd be 8 feet 10 inches.

The 6 feet 10 inch West Indian cricketer Joel Garner responds to an enquiry from a female supporter as to whether he is 'built in proportion', quoted in Simon Hughes, Yakking Round the World *(2000)*

He looks like he's got a *cheese danish* stuffed in his *pants*!

Tom Wolfe, The Bonfire of the Vanities *(1984)*

Q: Why do men have a hole in their penis?
A: So they can think with an open mind.

Anon.

Q: What's pink and hard in the morning?
A: The *Financial Times* crossword.

Anon.

Q: What can a bird do that a man can't?
A: Whistle through its pecker.

Anon.

Q: What did the elephant say to the naked man?
A: It's cute, but can you pick up peanuts with it?

Anon.

Q: Why are women so bad at parking?
A: Because men keep telling them that this [make a small gap between thumb and forefinger] is eight inches.

Anon.

Q: Why do moths fly with their legs apart?
A: Have you seen the size of moth balls?

Anon.

A Doctor writes:

TAKE EVERY PAIN IN INFANCY TO ENLARGE THE PRIVY MEMBER OF BOYS (BY MASSAGE AND THE APPLICATION OF STIMVLANTS), SINCE A WELL-GROWN SPECIMEN NEVER COMES AMISS.

GABRIELLO FALLOPIO, OBSERVATIONES ANATOMICAE *(1561)*

I think it's great if a guy has a good-sized package.
Janet Jackson

I'm hung like Einstein and smart as a horse.
Helmet sticker

Whenever a fellow called Rex
Flashed his very small organ of sex,
He always got off,
For the judges would scoff,
'De minimis non curat lex.'
(The law can't be bothered with tiny things)
Anon.

On penis envy:
I'm one of the few males who suffer from that.
Woody Allen as Alvy, in Annie Hall *(1977)*

Les crudités: genitals.
Andy Kirby, New Statesman *competition, 1985*

Appropriate response to a flasher who enquires 'What do you think of that, then?'

It's like a penis, only smaller.

Anon.

When you are said to be the f*** of the century it's a matter of course that every woman is disappointed after the first night with you. It's a fact that this adventure playground behind the zip of my trousers has myth status on the groupie scene.

Mick Jagger, quoted in the Observer, *21 September 2003*

Men think they can act like God Almighty because they've got a cock and they can mend a flex.

Victoria Wood

My Ding-a-Ling.

Chuck Berry, title of hit song

Q: Why do men think women have no brains?
A: Because they don't have any testicles to put them in.

Anon.

There once was a man from Madras
Who's balls were constructed of brass
When jangled together
They played 'Stormy Weather'
And lightning shot out of his ass.

Anon.

Hitler
Has only got one ball!
Goering
Has two, but very small!
Himmler
Has something similar,
But poor old Goebbels
Has no balls at all!

Anonymous World War II song, sung by British soldiers to the tune 'Colonel Bogey'. The 1945 Soviet autopsy report on Hitler noted 'In the scrotum, which is singed but preserved, only the right testicle was found. The left testicle could not be found in the inguinal canal.' How did all those soldiers know?

Sugar and Spice and All Things **NICE**

Clits, Twats and G-Spots

People will insist … on treating the *mons Veneris* as though it were Mount Everest.

Aldous Huxley, Eyeless in Gaza *(1936)*

She tilted her hips and felt the weight of his balls on her … what? Small expanse of skin between vagina and anus. Perineum – was that it? Her mind screamed: Shut up, Lucy! You're not doing the Cosmopolitan crossword now.

Nichola McAuliffe, The Crime Tsar *(2003)*

Q: What's the difference between a G-spot and a golf ball?
A: A guy will actually search for a golf ball.

Anon.

Finally, regarding hygiene, when Billy Wilder's wife complained from Paris just after World War II that there was no bidet, he cabled back:

```
UNABLE TO OBTAIN BIDET.
SUGGEST HANDSTAND IN SHOWER.
```

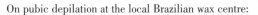

Q: What do a clitoris, a toilet and an anniversary have in common?
A: Men always miss them.

Anon.

On pubic depilation at the local Brazilian wax centre:

A woman pays hard cash to have her pubic hair ripped from her body so that she might then flaunt herself on Copacabana beach sporting a length of fluorescent dental floss between her labia.... If God had wanted us to spend our lives with our pussies looking like cold ham wrapped in clingfilm, we'd have been born that way, wouldn't we?

Rowena Raunchbitch, 'Torrid Sex Tips for Red-Hot Lovers', in The Rockall Times, *11 November 2002*

I know body hairs bother some women, but a lot of men like a fluffy partner.

Dame Edna Everage

Under her beauteous bosom there did lie
A belly as smooth as any ivory.
Yet nature to declare her various art
Had plac'd a tuft in one convenient part;
No park with smoothest lawn or highest wood
Could e'er compare with this admir'd abode.

Charles Sackville, Earl of Dorset, 'Duel of the Crabs'
(1701)

An' heard ye o the coat o arms
The Lyon brought our lady, O?
The crest was couchant sable cunt
The motto ready, ready, O,
Green grow the rashes, O
Green grow the rashes, O
The lassies they hae wimble-bores, good-tim
The widows they hae gashes, O

Robert Burns, 'Green Grow the Rashes, O'

Breasts, Busts and Gargantuan **GAZOONGAS**

'Big breaths, now.'
'Yeth, and I'm only thixteen.'

Richard Gordon, Doctor in the House

Without nipples, breasts would be pointless.

Jody Nathan

On the satisfactory nature of small breasts:

Anything more than a mouthful is wasted.

Anon.

If the effort that went into research on the female bosom had gone into our space program, we would now be running hot-dog stands on the moon.

Anon.

Q: What do electric trains and breasts have in common?
A: They're intended for children, but it's the men who end up playing with them.

Anon.

A grieving Australian widow has had her husband's ashes sewn into her breast implants, a British newspaper has reported. Sydney woman Sandi Canesco, 26, took the bizarre step after her new husband Dustin was killed in a car accident, downmarket tabloid the *Daily Star* said. 'It dawned on me that if I carried Dustin's cremated remains in my breast implants, I'd never really have to part with him at all, because then he and I would be one and the same,' the paper quoted Canesco as saying, under the headline 'Dust to bust'.

Weekend Australian

On meeting the Beckhams:

Victoria pointed to her necklace and said '£1.5 million.' David introduced himself. I was staring at his wife's tits and shouting 'How much?!'

Graham Norton

LEECHES COULD BURST JORDAN'S BOOBS

Doctors have warned that Jordan's 34FF breasts could explode if jungle leeches get to chomp on them. The silicone-enhanced glamour model plans to strip off on *I'm a Celebrity ... Get Me Out of Here ...*

Sky News, *22 January 2004*

I love her in her evening
  gown,
I love her in her nightie,
But when moonlight flits
Between her tits,
Oh my gawd, almighty!
Anon.

The only place men
want depth in a woman
is in her *décolletage.*
Zsa Zsa Gabor

DOLLY PARTON'S CLEAVAGE

I was the first woman to burn my bra – it took the fire department four days to put it out.

Dolly Parton

Dolly Parton has a yacht in Seattle and it's windy there. One day she hung up her bra to dry and woke up in Brazil.

Phyllis Diller

It was a fantastic, surreal sight. They looked like two boiled eggs in blue eggcups. Their pates gleamed in unison … If you'd stuck a few sequins on their heads they'd have looked like Dolly Parton's cleavage.

Simon Hoggart describes Conservative leader Ian Duncan Smith and his similarly follically challenged predecessor William Hague at the 2001 Conservatory Party conference. Sketch, 'A Right Pair of Dolly Partons', in the Guardian, *10 October 2001.*

Posterior
RESOURCES

The Bottom

Of Marilyn Monroe:

There's a broad with her future behind her.

Constance Bennett

There was a young lady of Eton
Whose figure had plenty of meat on.
She said, 'Marry me, dear,
And you'll find that my rear
Is a nice place to warm your cold feet on.'

Anon.

J-LO'S BOTTOM:

IT WAS THE SUN WOT CRACKED IT

Spoof headline in BBC Radio 4's Absolute Power, *with Stephen Fry and John Bird, 5 February 2004*

Who says we shouldn't be fat? Who says you shouldn't have a big bottom?

Victoria Wood, quoted in the Observer, *30 November 2003*

The breasts of a barmaid of Crail
Were tattooed with the price of brown ale,
While on her behind
For the sake of the blind
Was the same information in Braille.

Anon.

*Colleague, running his hand over the bald head
of the US politician Nicholas Longworth
(1869–1931):* It feels just like my wife's behind.
Longworth: Why, so it does.

There was a young girl of Madras
Who had the most beautiful ass.
But not as you'd think
Firm, round and pink,
But grey, with long ears and eats grass.

Anon.

Asked which part of her body she would change:

**I wouldn't change anything, but I could
do with sharing my bottom and thighs
with at least two other people.**

Christine Hamilton, quoted in the Observer, *4 April 2004*

Legs
(Up to the Armpit or Otherwise)

There was a young spinster from Ealing
Endowed with such delicate feeling
That she thought that a chair
Shouldn't have its legs bare
So she kept her eyes fixed on the ceiling.

Anon.

The average man is more interested in a woman
who is interested in him than he is in a woman –
any woman – with beautiful legs.

Marlene Dietrich, in 1954

The female knee is a joint, and not an entertainment.

Percy Hammond, reviewing a musical in the Chicago Tribune,
c.1912

– Her legs are without equal.
– You mean they know no parallel.

Anon.

You were born with your legs apart. They'll send
you to the grave in a Y-shaped coffin.

Joe Orton, What the Butler Saw *(1967)*

The word today is *Legs* ... Spread the word.

Anon.

Come Again?
Double
ENTENDRES

She touched his organ, and from that bright
epoch even it, the old companion of his happiest
hours, incapable as he had thought of elevation,
began a new and defined existence.

Charles Dickens, Martin Chuzzlewit *(1843–4)*

There was an old man of Boulogne
Who sang a most topical song;
It wasn't the words
That frightened the birds
But the terrible double ontong.

Anon.

Would you, my dear young friends, like to be
inside with the five wise virgins, or outside, alone,
and in the dark, with the five foolish ones?

*Henry Montagu Butler (1833–1918), attributed. Butler was
headmaster of Harrow, then master of Trinity College, Cambridge.*

There is nothing I like better than to lie on my bed for an hour with my favourite Trollope.

Unnamed Bishop of Bath and Wells, quoted in Chips Channon's diary for 4 April 1943

It takes a hell of a lot for a man to put up with me. I can be a handful.

Jordan

SOME UNFORTUNATE BOOK TITLES

BRITISH TITS

A suggestive ornithological survey from Christopher Perrins in 1979

SHAG THE CARIBOU

A 1949 wildlife book for children by C. Bernard Rutley

FLASHES FROM THE WELSH PULPIT

1889 book title published by Hodder & Stoughton

MAKING IT IN LEATHER

DIY title by M. Vincent Hayes from 1972

WHAT DO BUNNIES DO ALL DAY?

A searching inquiry by Judy Mastrangelo (1988)

LICKEY END AND OTHER PUNNING PLACE NAMES

Nobber (Donegal, Ireland)

Arsoli (Lazio, Italy)

Muff (Northern Ireland)

Twatt (Shetland, UK)

Dildo (Newfoundland, Canada)

Wankie (Zimbabwe)

Climax (Colorado, USA)

Lickey End (West Midlands, UK)

Shafter (California, USA)

Intercourse (Pennsylvania, USA)

Brown Willy (every schoolboy's favourite, Cornwall, UK)

Fukue (Honshu, Japan)

Shag Island (Indian Ocean)

Sexmoan (Luzon, Philippines)

Wet Beaver Creek (Australia)

Chinaman's Knob (Australia)

A BIT OF GENTLE BONDAGE

Pussy: My name is Pussy Galore.
Bond: I must be dreaming.
Line from the film version of Goldfinger *(1964)*

Aki (to Bond): I think I will enjoy very much serving under you.
Line from the film version of You Only Live Twice *(1967)*

Lot: The Sodomite cavalry are notoriously unreliable.
Line from the film Sodom and Gomorrah *(1962)*

I am part man, part cyborg. You'd be surprised at the parts I've had inserted in me. Perhaps that's why I walk a little stiffly.
Graham Norton

I'd love to pour my hot milky drink into your mug.
Graham Norton to French footballing pin-up David Ginola, on So Graham Norton, *2 March 2001. An admiring Norton was describing the use to which he would like to put an Aston Villa mug adorned with Ginola's face.*

Howard's End? Sounds filthy, doesn't it?
Willy Russell, film version of Educating Rita *(1983)*

OOPS! REGRETTABLE HEADLINES THROUGH THE AGES

Student excited dad got head job

6B • THE UNIVERSITY DAILY KANSAN SPORTS

EIGHTH ARMY PUSH BOTTLES UP GERMANS

Possibly apocryphal British newspaper headline during World War II

ANTIQUE STRIPPER TO DISPLAY WARES AT STORE

MRS RYDELL'S BUST UNVEILED AT NEARBY SCHOOL

SOVIET VIRGIN LANDS SHORT OF GOAL AGAIN

NUNS DROP SUIT; BISHOPS AGREE TO AID THEM

PASTOR AGHAST AFTER FIRST LADY SEX POSITION

MRS CORSON'S SEAT UP FOR GRABS

ORGAN FESTIVAL ENDS IN SMASHING CLIMAX

IS THERE A RING OF DEBRIS AROUND URANUS?

WOMAN OFF TO JAIL FOR SEX WITH BOYS

The Record, *23 October 1984*

BONNIE BLOWS CLINTON

Headline in the Sampson Independent, *27 August, 1998. Bonnie is a hurricane, Clinton a town in North Carolina.*

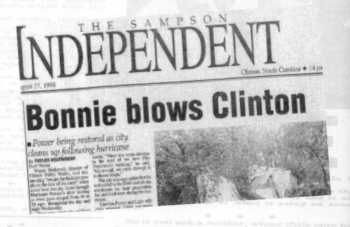

Julius II (to Michelangelo): You dare to dicker with your pontiff?

Line from the film The Agony and the Ecstasy *(1965), from the novel by Irving Stone*

Every prime minister needs a Willie.

Margaret Thatcher, speech on the occasion of William Whitelaw's retirement, 1989

I'm not *against* half-naked girls – not as often as I'd like to be …

Benny Hill, The Benny Hill Show, *1984*

To a female cellist:

You have between your legs the most sensitive instrument known to man, and all you can do is to sit there and scratch it.

Sir Thomas Beecham

A WARM HAND ON YOUR OPENING

Noël Coward, telegram to the actress Gertrude Lawrence on an opening night

ALWAYS HOT AND ALWAYS READY

Sign outside fish-and-chip shop

Dating, Wooing and Generally Trying **IT ON**

Nothing risqué, nothing gained.

Alexander Woollcott

QUOD IUVAT, INVITAE SAEPE DEDISSE VOLVNT.
(Whether they give or refuse, women are
delighted to have been asked.)

OVID, THE ART OF LOVE

For when success a lover's toil attends,
Few ask, if fraud or force attain'd his ends.

Alexander Pope, *The Rape of the Lock* (1712–14)

Sex is better than talk ... Talk is what you suffer
through so you can get to sex.

Woody Allen

You have to penetrate a woman's defences.
Getting into her head is a prerequisite to getting
into her body.

Bob Guccione, publisher of Penthouse *magazine*

I wasn't being free with my hands – I was trying to guess her weight.

W.C. Fields

Give a man a free hand, and you'll know where to find it.

Mae West

You know that look women get when they want sex? Me neither.

Steve Martin

When a man goes on a date, he wonders if he is going to get lucky. A woman already knows.

Frederike Ryder

If you ask for a doggy bag on a date, you might as well wrap up your genitals too, because you're not going to be needing them for a long time.

Jerry Seinfeld

Take not the first refusal ill:
Tho' now she won't, anon she will.

Thomas D'Urfey

Q: How do men exercise at the beach?
A: By sucking in their stomachs every time they see a bikini.

Anon.

Men generally pay for all expenses on a date ...
Either sex, however, may bring a little gift, its
value to be determined by the bizarreness of the
sexual request to be made later that evening.

P.J. O'Rourke, *Modern Manners (1983)*

Sweet Sir Walter

*Sir Walter Raleigh loved a wench well; and one time
getting up one of the maids of honour up against a
tree in a wood who at first boarding to be somewhat
fearful of her honour, and modest, she cried 'Sweet
Sir Walter, what do you me ask? Will you undo me?
Nay, sweet Sir Walter! Sweet Sir Walter! Sir
Walter! Sir Walter!' At last, as the danger and the
pleasure at the same time grew higher, she cried in
the ecstasy, 'Swisser Swatter, Swisser Swatter!'*

John Aubrey, *Brief Lives* (17th century)

Sex is like snow, you never know how many inches
you're going to get or how long it will last.

Anon.

A girl's legs are her best friends, but the best of
friends must part.

Redd Foxx

A date, at this juncture in history, is any prearranged meeting with the opposite sex toward whom you have indecent intentions … One does not have to sleep with, or even touch, someone who has paid for your meal. All those obligations are hereby rendered null and void, and any man who doesn't think so needs a quick jab in the kidney.

Cynthia Heimel, Sex Tips for Girls *(1983)*

may i feel said he
(i'll squeal said she
just once said he)
it's fun said she
(may i touch said he
how much said she
a lot said he)
why not said she
(let's go said he
not too far said she
what's too far said he
where you are said she)

e.e. cummings, 'may i feel said he'

Had we but world enough, and time,
This coyness, lady, were no crime.

Andrew Marvell, 'To His Coy Mistress'

I love those slow-talking Southern girls. I was out with a Southern girl last night, took her so long to tell me she wasn't that kind of girl, she was.

Woody Woodbury

There are three possible parts to a date, of which at least two must be offered: entertainment, food, and affection. It is customary to begin a series of dates with a great deal of entertainment, a moderate amount of food, and the merest suggestion of affection. As the amount of affection increases, the entertainment can be reduced proportionately. When the affection *is* the entertainment, we no longer call it dating. Under no circumstances can the food be omitted.

Miss Manners' Guide to Excruciatingly Correct Behaviour

To succeed with the opposite sex, tell her you're impotent. She can't wait to disprove it.

Cary Grant

Chat-Ups and
PUT-DOWNS

I don't believe we've met. I'm Mr Right.

A line suggested by Playboy *in 1969*

Bend over, I'll drive.

Bumper sticker

I may not be Fred Flintstone, but I can make your bed rock.

Anon.

Mrs Teasdale (gushingly): Oh your excellency!
Firefly: You're not so bad yourself.

Lines from Duck Soup *(1933)*

Bond: What gives?
Miss Moneypenny: Me – given half a chance.

Lines from Dr No *(1962)*

Q: What did Big Ben say to the Leaning Tower of Pisa?
A: I've got the time if you've got the inclination.

Anon.

*This sublime age reduces everything to its quintessence;
all periphrases and expletives are so much in disuse, that
I suppose soon the only way to making love will be to say
'Lie down.'*

Horace Walpole, letter to H.S. Conway, 23 October 1778

And, to illustrate the point:

When I first met my girlfriend, she asked me what
I wanted in a woman. She pretended to be
irritated when I said, 'My dick.'

Anon.

There was the one about the doctor ... He was
examining a girl's knee and he said, 'What's a joint
like this doing in a pretty girl like you?'

Line from the film Kiss Me Stupid *(1964)*

If I said you had a beautiful body would you hold
it against me?

Anon.

Shall we shag now, or shall we shag later?

Line from Austin Powers *(1997)*

I told her the thing I loved most about her was her
mind ... because that's what told her to get into
bed with me naked.

Steven Wright

You know, I've been wanting to go out with you ever since I read the stuff on the men's bathroom wall two years ago.

Anon.

I want to feel my way along you, all over you and up and down you and in and out … I want to be reincarnated as your tampon.

Prince Charles, purported phone conversation with Camilla Parker-Bowles, December 1989

MAKE LOVE NOT WAR (see driver for details)

Bumper sticker

My ultimate fantasy is to entice a man to my bedroom, put a gun to his head and say, 'Make babies or die.'

Ruby Wax

Bond: My dear girl, don't flatter yourself. What I did this evening was for king and country. You don't think it gave me any pleasure, do you?

Line from film version of Thunderball *(1965)*

Bud: You know what we're going to do after dinner?
Fran: The dishes?

Lines from The Apartment *(1960), screenplay by Billy Wilder and I.A.L. Diamond*

Whenever I go to a bar, I always go right up to the most beautiful woman in the room and say:
'You've got something hanging out of your nose.'
Hey, since I've got no shot at her, I might as well humble her a little for the next guy.

Michael Hayward

If y'all can hold it in one hand, I ain't the least bit interested.

Anon.

Act your age, not your size.

Anon.

When the vertically challenged star Mickey Rooney suggested to a tall chorus girl that he have sex with her, she replied:

All right, but if you do and I ever get to hear about it, I'll be very, very cross indeed.

Is it in?

Anon.

Well, what you lack in size, you make up for in speed.

Anon.

TOP TEN REJECTION LINES DELIVERED BY WOMEN

1. **I think of you as a brother** = You remind me of that inbred banjo-playing geek in *Deliverance*.

2. **There's a slight difference in our ages** = You are one Jurassic geezer.

3. **I'm not attracted to you in that way** = You are the ugliest dork I've ever laid eyes on.

4. **My life is too complicated right now** = I don't want you spending the whole night or you may hear phone calls from all the other guys I'm seeing.

5. **I've got a boyfriend** = I've got my male cat and a half gallon of Ben & Jerry's ice-cream.

6. **I don't date men where I work** = Hey, bud, I wouldn't even date you if you were in the same solar system, much less the same building.

7. **It's not you, it's me** = It's not me, it's you.

8. **I'm concentrating on my career** = Even something as boring and unfulfilling as my job is better than dating you.

9. **I'm celibate** = I've sworn off only the men like you.

10. **Let's be friends** = I want you to stay around so that I can tell you in excruciating detail about all the other men I meet and have sex with – it's that male perspective thing.

I've had a wonderful evening, but this wasn't it.

Groucho Marx

A girl phoned me the other day and said, 'Come on over, there's nobody home.' I went over. Nobody was home.

Rodney Dangerfield

Do the words 'sex' and 'travel' mean anything to you? Good: now FUCK OFF!

Anon.

I'm not your type. I'm not inflatable.

Anon.

This guy says, 'I'm perfect for you, 'cause I'm a cross between a macho and a sensitive man.' I said, 'Oh, a gay trucker?'

Judy Tenuta

An adventurous fun-loving polyp
Propositioned a cute little scallop
Down under the sea.
'Nothing doing,' said she;
'By Triton, you think I'm a trollop.'

Anon.

TOP TEN REJECTION LINES DELIVERED BY MEN

1. **I think of you as a sister** = You're ugly.
2. **There's a slight difference in our ages** = You're ugly.
3. **I'm not attracted to you in that way** = You're ugly.
4. **My life is too complicated right now** = You're ugly.
5. **I've got a girlfriend** = You're ugly.
6. **I don't date women where I work** = You're ugly.
7. **It's not you, it's me** = You're ugly.
8. **I'm concentrating on my career** = You're ugly.
9. **I'm celibate** = You're ugly.
10. **Let's be friends** = You're sinfully ugly.

There was a young actress from Crewe,
Who remarked, as the vicar withdrew,
'The Bishop was quicker
And thicker and slicker,
And two inches longer than you.'
Anon.

Good-Time
GIRLS (and Boys)

She was the original good time that was had by all.

Bette Davis, referring to a now-forgotten starlet

She's been on more laps than a napkin.

Walter Winchell

I admit, I have a tremendous sex drive. My boyfriend lives forty miles away.

Phyllis Diller

The Grand Old Duchess of York,
She had ten thousand men.
She'd march them up to the top of the hill,
Then say, 'Go on, do it again!'

Anon.

It's impossible to ravish me,
I'm so willing.

John Fletcher, *The Faithful Shepherdess* (1610)

Would you like to sin
With Eleanor Glynn
On a tiger skin?
Or would you prefer
To err
With her
On some other fur?

Anon. Ms Glynn was an actress in the early decades of the 20th century, and regarded as somewhat 'fast'.

Firefly: Remember, you're fighting for this woman's honour – which is more than she ever did.

Line from Duck Soup *(1933)*

If you still have the same shears, Delilah, my hair's rather long.

Lecherous Philistine in the 1949 film Samson and Delilah

Of Queen Caroline's alleged adultery with the dey (governor) of Algiers:

She was happy as the dey was long.

Chief Justice Lord Norbury, at Queen Caroline's trial in the House of Lords, 1820

Your idea of fidelity is not having more than one man in the bed at the same time.

Dirk Bogarde to Julie Christie in Darling *(1965), screenplay by Frederic Raphael*

The Professor of Gynaecology began his course of lectures as follows: Gentlemen, woman is an animal that micturates once a day, defecates once a week, menstruates once a month, parturates once a year and copulates whenever she has the opportunity.

W. Somerset Maugham, A Writer's Notebook *(1949)*

I like the girls who do,
I like the girls who don't;
I hate the girl who says she will
And then she says she won't.
But the girl that I like best of all
And I think you'll say I'm right –
Is the one who says she never has
But looks as though she …
'Ere, listen …

Max Miller

A mistress comes between a mister and his mattress.

Anon.

Kathy Sue Loudermilk was a lovely child and a legend before her sixteenth birthday. She was twenty-one, however, before she knew an automobile had a front seat.

Lewis Grizzard

There was a little girl
Who had a little curl
Right in the middle of her forehead,
When she was good she was very very good
And when she was bad she was very very popular.

Max Miller

Good girls go to heaven.
But bad girls go everywhere.

Helen Gurley Brown, Sex and the Single Girl *(1963)*

Lady Rumpers: And then you took me.
Sir Percy: I took *you*? You took *me*. Your Land
Army breeches came down with a fluency born of
long practice.

Alan Bennett, Habeas Corpus *(1973)*

I loved Kirk so much I would have skied down
Mount Everest in the nude with a carnation up my
nose.

*Joyce McKinney, the former Miss Wyoming who abducted a
Mormon missionary, Kirk Anderson, chained him to the bed and
forced him to have sex with her. She made this remark at her trial
in Epsom on 6 December 1977.*

What men desire is a virgin who is a whore.

Edward Dahlberg, Reasons of the Heart *(1965)*

THE RATIO OF WIT TO CHASTITY

I am sorry to say that the generality of women who have excelled in wit have failed in chastity.

Elizabeth Montagu.

And, to prove the point …

Ducking for apples – change one letter and it's the story of my life.

Dorothy Parker

Tell him I've been too fucking busy – or vice versa.

Dorothy Parker, on her honeymoon, when her editor (Harold Ross of The New Yorker*) was badgering her for overdue copy*

If all the young ladies who attended the Yale promenade dance were laid end to end, no one would be the least surprised.

Dorothy Parker

So many men, so little time.

Mae West

You know, she speaks eighteen languages.
And she can't say 'No' in any of them.
Dorothy Parker

It's not the men in my life, but the life in my men.
Mae West, in I'm No Angel *(1933)*

When I'm good I'm very good, but when I'm bad I'm better.
Mae West, in I'm No Angel *(1933)*

When women go wrong, men go right after them.
Mae West

My girlfriend can count all the lovers she's had on one hand – if she's holding a calculator.
Tom Cotter

Q: What's the difference between a bitch and a whore?
A: A whore sleeps with everybody at the party and a bitch sleeps with everybody at the party except you.
Anon.

Advice to young women:

Don't screw around, and don't smoke.

Edwina Currie, then a junior health minister, quoted in the Observer, *3 April 1988. This was after her own affair with John Major.*

Nymphomaniac: a woman as obsessed with sex as an average man.

Mignon McLaughlin, The Neurotic's Notebook *(1960)*

Elyot: It doesn't suit women to be promiscuous.
Amanda: It doesn't suit men for women to be promiscuous.

Noël Coward, Private Lives *(1930)*

What is a promiscuous person? It's usually someone who is getting more sex than you are.

Victor Lownes, manager of the American Playboy Club

Vanity, revenge, loneliness, boredom, all apply: lust is one of the least of the reasons for promiscuity.

Mignon McLaughlin, The Second Neurotic's Notebook *(1966)*

Most of the busy love-makers I knew were looking for masculinity rather than practising it. They were fellows of dubious lust.

Ben Hecht, A Child of the Century *(1954)*

We all know girls do it. But if you ask them to do it, they say no. Why? Because they want to be proper. Finally, after thirteen years of courtship and dates and so on, one night they get drunk and they do it. And *after* they've done it, that's all they want to do. Now they're fallen, now they're disgraced, and all they want is to do it. You say, 'Let's have a cup of tea.' 'No, let's do it.' 'Let's go to the cinema.' 'No, let's do it.'

Mel Brooks, quoted in Time Out, *1984*

BLONDES

It was a blonde, a blonde to make a bishop kick a hole in a stained-glass window.
Raymond Chandler, Farewell My Lovely *(1940)*

Gentlemen prefer blondes.
Anita Loos, book title (1925)

It's also possible that blondes prefer gentlemen.
Mamie Van Doren

It's great being blonde – with such low expectations it's easy to impress.
Pamela Anderson

I have been more ravished myself than any body since the Trojan War.

Lord Byron, letter, 29 October 1819

The trouble with life is that there are so many beautiful women and so little time.

John Barrymore

Of Ian Fleming, creator of James Bond:

The trouble with Ian is that he gets off with women because he can't get on with them.

Rosamond Lehmann

If you want to know the secret of my success with women, then don't smoke, don't take drugs and don't be too particular.

George Best

When from time to time I have seen the persons with whom the great lovers satisfied their desires, I have often been more astonished by the robustness of their appetites than envious of their success. It is obvious that you need not often go hungry if you are willing to dine off mutton hash and turnip tops.

W. Somerset Maugham, The Summing Up *(1938)*

I am always looking for meaningful one night stands.

Dudley Moore

Of his many girlfriends:

The most memorable one is always the current one; the rest just merge into a sea of blondes.

Rod Stewart. On another occasion he observed: 'Instead of getting married again, I'm going to find a woman I don't like and just give her a house.'

I am always crazy for hot women. I am like a rabbit. I could do it any time, anywhere.

Rod Stewart

HAIL THE CONQUERING HERO COMES …

AMONG THE MANY HONOURS THAT OUR YOUNG MEN CAN WIN FOR DISTINGUISHED SERVICE IN WAR WILL BE MORE FREQUENT OPPORTUNITIES TO SLEEP WITH WOMEN.

PLATO, *REPUBLIC*

Against this may be placed the slogan of US draft resisters during the Vietnam War:

GIRLS SAY YES TO GUYS WHO SAY NO.

He had ambitions, at one time, to become a sex maniac, but he failed his practical.

Les Dawson

Never miss a chance to have sex or be on television.

Gore Vidal

IT'S PADDY PANTSDOWN

The Sun *newspaper in 1992, on the admission of an extra-marital affair by Paddy Ashdown, leader of the Liberal Democrats (1988–99)*

To a woman whom he had served well:

Don't thank me. Tell your friends.

Michael Vermeulen, late publisher of GQ, *quoted in the* Independent, *2 September 1995*

I am the only man who can say he's been in Take That and at least two members of the Spice Girls.

Robbie Williams

It would be less demanding, enslaving, perplexing and strenuous for a healthy male to screw a thousand women in his lifetime than to try to please one, and the potential for failure would be less.

Irma Kurtz

'Has it ever occurred to you that in your promiscuous pursuit of women you are merely trying to assuage your subconscious fears of sexual impotence?'

'Yes, sir, it has.'

'They why do you do it?'

'To assuage my subconscious fears of sexual impotence.'

Joseph Heller, Catch-22 *(1961)*

Love Goddesses of Stage AND SCREEN

Suggested epitaph for an unnamed screen goddess:

She sleeps alone at last.

Robert Benchley

It's the good girls that keep the diaries; the bad girls never have the time

Tallulah Bankhead

I like to wake up feeling a new man.

Jean Harlow

When Jean Harlow asked Margot Asquith how to pronounce her first name, the latter replied:

'Margo' – the T is silent, as in 'Harlow'.

On being told that ten men were waiting outside her dressing room:

I'm tired, send one of them home.

Mae West

From the moment I was six I felt sexy. And let me tell you it was hell, sheer hell, waiting to do something about it.

Bette Davis

I used to be Snow White, but I drifted.

Mae West

I live by a man's code, designed to fit a man's world, yet at the same time I never forgot that a woman's first job is to choose the right shade of lipstick.

Carole Lombard

I knew at once that Rock Hudson was gay when he did not fall in love with me.

Gina Lollobrigida

I've been around so long, I knew Doris Day before she was a virgin.

Groucho Marx

Doris Day is as wholesome as a bowl of cornflakes and at least as sexy.

Dwight MacDonald

It's not true that I had nothing on. I had the radio on.

Marilyn Monroe. On another occasion, on being asked what she wore in bed, she replied, 'Chanel No. 5'.

On Marilyn Monroe as Sugar:

Look at that! Look how she moves! It's just like Jell-O on springs … I tell you, it's a whole different sex.

Jerry (Jack Lemmon) to Joe (Tony Curtis) in Some Like It Hot *(1959)*

On love scenes with Marilyn Monroe:

It's like kissing Hitler.

Tony Curtis. (Helena Bonham Carter later observed that kissing Woody Allen was 'like kissing the Berlin Wall'.)

Copulation was, I'm sure, Marilyn's uncomplicated way of saying thank you.

Nunnally Johnson, film director and producer, on Marilyn Monroe

It is better to be unfaithful than to be faithful without wanting to be.

Brigitte Bardot

I haven't had a hit film since Joan Collins was a virgin.

Burt Reynolds, quoted in the Observer, *27 March 1988*

On being dropped by the Earl of Lichfield because she was 'no good in the country':

And he's no good in bed.

Britt Ekland

Acting is like sex. You should do it, not talk about it.

Joanne Woodward

I'm finished with men, but I have a very full memory.

Ursula Andress, quoted in the Observer, *7 January 1996. Her conquests are said to have included Marlon Brando, James Dean, Elvis Presley and Ryan O'Neal.*

My dad told me, 'Anything worth having is worth waiting for.' I waited until I was 15.

Zsa Zsa Gabor

The important thing in acting is to be able to laugh and cry. If I have to cry I think of my sex life. If I have to laugh, I think of my sex life.

Glenda Jackson

I guess a film in which I didn't end up in bed, in the sea or in a hot tub would have the same appeal as a Clint Eastwood movie in which nobody got shot.

Bo Derek, quoted in the Independent, *25 March 1995*

I have to get out before I become the grotesque caricature of the hatchet-faced woman with big knockers.

Jamie Lee Curtis

If you have a vagina and an attitude in this town, then that's a lethal combination.

Sharon Stone, quoted in Empire, *June 1992*

The movie business divides women into ice queens and sluts, and there have been times I wanted to be a slut more than anything.

Sigourney Weaver

What's nice about my dating life is that I don't have to leave the house. All I have to do is read the paper: I'm marrying Richard Gere, dating Daniel Day-Lewis ... and even Robert de Niro was in there for a day.

Julia Roberts

Underneath all this drag, I'm really a librarian, you know.

Bette Midler

I carried my Oscar to bed with me. My first and only three-way happened that night.

Halle Berry

Everyone probably thinks I'm a raving nymphomaniac, that I have an insatiable sexual appetite, when the truth is I'd rather read a book.

Madonna, quoted in Q Magazine, *June 1991*

I don't know how long it takes to become a virgin again, but I think I'm half way there.

Pamela Anderson, quoted in the Observer, *5 October 2003*

Some men send me condoms and underpants. I'm not sure what they want.

Martine McCutcheon

SOME GAY ICONS

I think the longer I look good, the better gay men feel.

Cher

Gay icons usually have some tragedy in their lives, but I've only had tragic haircuts and outfits.

Kylie Minogue

The homosexual community wants me to be gay. The heterosexual community wants me to be straight ... I pray that they get a life and stop living mine.

Ricky Martin

I like exposing myself. There's not an awful lot that embarrasses me. I'm the kind of actress who absolutely believes in exposing herself.

Kate Winslet

You've all heard some rumours about me over the years. I guess this is the moment to do it. My name is Richard Gere and I am a lesbian.

Richard Gere

And, finally, some Love Gods:

My trouble is reconciling my gross habits with my net income.

Errol Flynn

Is it a man walking on the beach, winking at the girls and looking for going to bed? Is it someone who wears a lot of gold chains and rings and sits at the bar? Because this is not me! I am very, very Latin, but not so much lover.

Antonio Banderas

On suggestions regarding his relationships:

Sometimes its Britney Spears and sometimes it's Carrie Fisher. I can't tell if I've got a Lolita complex or an Oedipus complex.

Ben Affleck

Aphrodisiacs

Liquor is Quicker

One more drink and I'll be under
the host.

Dorothy Parker

*It provokes the desire, but it takes
away the performance. Therefore
much drink may be said to be an
equivocator with lechery.*

William Shakespeare, *Macbeth* (1605)

Beer: helping fat ugly people
get laid since 1735.

Spoof slogan

For women the best
aphrodisiacs are words. The
G-spot is in the ears. He who looks for it below
there is wasting his time.

Isabel Allende

Oysters is amorous,
Lobsters is lecherous,
But shrrrimps, Chrrrrist,
When my old man came 'ome last night …

Anon. (c.1940s)

Women find men who have a sense of humour
EXTREMELY SEXY! You don't have to look like
Robert Redford. All you have to do is tickle her
funny bone, and she'll follow you anywhere! If you
can make her laugh, you've got it made!

Man: One to call her Dad and the other to open
the Diet Pepsi!
Woman: Oh stop! You're KILLING me! Take off all
your clothes quick!

Mimi Pond, Mimi Pond's Secrets of the Powder Room *(1983)*

Power is the great aphrodisiac.

Henry Kissinger, quoted in The New York Times, *19 January
1971. His one-time companion, Barbara Howar, commented:
'Henry's idea of sex is to slow down to 30 miles an hour when he
drops you off at the door.'*

A Vision in Pink writes:

The right diet directs sexual energy into the parts
that matter.

Barbara Cartland, quoted in the Observer, *11 January 1981*

A CHOICE OF STIMULANTS

Various texts over the centuries from a variety of cultures around the world have proposed a whole host of substances to increase libido and enhance desire. Among these one might draw particular attention to:

- The testicles of a hare
- The penis of a donkey
- The secretions from the vagina of a pig
- Bull's piss
- Hen's excrement
- The blood and brains of a sparrow
- Mandrake root in the shape of a penis
- Blood from a man's pinkie taken in a woman's wine
- A snake squashed by an elephant as it expires
- Young men's semen mixed with the excrement of a falcon

Girls have been known to go to a graveyard at night, exhume a corpse that had been nine days buried, and tear down a strip of the skin from head to foot; this they manage to tie round the leg or arm of the man they love while he sleeps, taking care to remove it before his awakening. And so long as the girl keeps this strip of skin in her possession, secretly hidden from all eyes, so long will she retain the man's love.

Lady Wilde ('Speranza'), Ancient Cures, Charms and Usages of Ireland *(1890)*

Aristotle was in no doubt as to the Viagra *de ses jours*:

ERECTION IS CHIEFLY CAUSED BY SCURAUM, ERYNGOES, CRESSES, CRYMON, PARSNIPS, ARTICHOKES, TURNIPS, ASPARAGUS, CANDIED GINGER, ACORNS BRUISED TO POWDER AND DRUNK IN MUSCATEL, SCALLION, SEA SHELLFISH, ETCETERA.
ARISTOTLE, *THE MASTERPIECE* (4TH CENTURY BC)

Au contraire:

WOOD PIGEONS CHECK AND BLUNT THE MANLY POWERS; LET HIM NOT EAT THE BIRD WHO WISHES TO BE AMOROUS.
MARTIAL, *EPIGRAMS* (C.AD 90)

Kissing, Necking, Spooning ...
FORKING?

Whoever named it necking was a poor judge of anatomy.

Groucho Marx

A Doctor writes (stating the obvious while missing the point):

One special form of contact which consists of mutual approximation of the mucous membranes of the lips in a kiss has received a sexual value among the civilized nations, though the parts of the body do not belong to the sexual apparatus and merely form the entrance to the digestive tract.

Sigmund Freud

We did one of those quick, awkward kisses where each of you gets a nose in the eye.

Clive James, Unreliable Memoirs *(1980)*

It takes a lot of experience for a girl to kiss like a beginner.

Ladies' Home Journal, *1948*

There was a young woman of Thrace
Whose nose spread all over her face.
She had very few kisses,
The reason for this is
There wasn't a suitable place.

Anon.

Her kisses left something to be desired – the rest of her.

Anon.

There was an old spinster from Fife
Who had never been kissed in her life.
Along came a cat
And she said, 'I'll kiss that,'
But the cat meowed, 'Not on your life!'

Anon.

Accused by his wife of kissing a chorus girl:

But I wasn't kissing her, I was whispering in her mouth.

Chico Marx

Kissing don't last: cookery do!

George Meredith, The Ordeal of Richard Feverel *(1859)*

She frowned and called him 'Mr'
Because in sport he kr.
And so in spite,
That very night
That Mr kr sr.
Anon.

Of Mick Jagger:
With those lips, he could kiss a moose.
Joan Rivers

**Where do
the noses go?
I always
wondered
where the
noses would go.**
Ernest Hemingway, For
Whom the Bell Tolls
(1940)

Playing
PRELUDES

Foreplay

See also Bad Sex; Tips on Technique.

There was a young student called Jones
Who'd reduce any maiden to moans
By his wonderful knowledge
Acquired in college
Of nineteen erogenous zones.

Anon.

Women are like ovens. We need five to fifteen
minutes to heat up.

Sandra Bullock

Q: Why don't women blink during foreplay?
A: They don't have time.

Anon.

Q: What's a man's idea of foreplay?
A: Half an hour of begging.

Anon.

One of the great breakthroughs in sex has been the discovery of all the new erogenous zones. Once it was thought there were only a handful. Now they are all over the place, with new ones being reported every day. Don't try to go at too many at once. If you do, they will cancel one another out, with some of the traditional old-line ones being neutralized. A sensitive partner can help by tapping you on the shoulder and saying, 'You are tackling too many erogenous zones.'

Bruce Jay Friedman, 'Sex and the Lonely Guy', in Esquire *(1977)*

Foreplay is like beefburgers – three minutes each side.

Victoria Wood

For flavour, instant sex will never supersede the stuff you have to peel and cook.

Quentin Crisp

He twisted my nipples as though tuning a radio.

Lisa Alther, Kinflicks *(1976)*

Q: Why do so many women fake orgasm?
A: Because so many men fake foreplay.

Anon.

MORE WORDS FROM THE WISE

LET THERE BE LEWD TOUCHING FIRST AND GAMES
BEFORE THE WORK.
ANON. GREEK (5TH CENTURY BC)

*A man must hug, and dandle, and kittle, and play
a hundred little tricks with his bed-fellow when he is
disposed to make that use of her that nature designed
her for.*
Erasmus, *Praise of Folly* (1509)

*License my roving hands, and let them go,
Before, behind, between, above, below.*
John Donne, 'To His Mistress Going to Bed' (c.1595)

The Fifties was the most sexually frustrated
decade ever: ten years of foreplay.
Lily Tomlin

Erections and Other Feats of **ENGINEERING**

The angle of the dangle is proportional to the heat of the meat provided that the urge to surge remains constant.

Anon.

A hard man's good to find – but you'll mostly find him asleep.

Mae West

Is that a gun in your pocket or are you just pleased to see me?

Mae West

An erection at will is the moral equivalent of a valid credit card.

Alex Comfort

The difference between light and hard is that you can sleep with a light on.

Anon.

Stand, stately Tavie, out of the codpiece rise,
And dig a grave between thy mistress' thighs;
Swift stand, then stab 'till she replies,
Then gently weep, and after weeping die.
Stand, Tavie, and gain thy credit lost;
Or by this hand I'll never draw thee, but against a post.

Anon. (18th century)

An erection is like the Theory of Relativity – the more you think about it, the harder it gets.

Anon.

Men wake up aroused in the morning. We can't help it. We just wake up and we want you. And the women are thinking, 'How can he want me the way I look in the morning?' It's because we can't see you. We have no blood anywhere near our optic nerve.

Andy Rooney

Sex is more fun than cars but cars refuel quicker than men.

Germaine Greer

There's a new medical crisis. Doctors are reporting that many men are having allergic reactions to latex condoms. They say they cause severe swelling. So what's the problem?

Phyllis Diller

Lying Limp and Coming **QUICK**

See also Bad Sex; Geriatric Sex.

Didst thou e'er fail in all thy life before?
When vile disease and scandal lead the way
With what officious haste dost thou obey.
But when great Love the onset does command
Base recreant to thy Prime, thou dar'st not stand …

John Wilmot, Earl of Rochester, 'The Imperfect Enjoyment' (1680)

Do we have any impotent men in here tonight?
Oh, I see, you can't get your arms up either.

Roseanne Barr

There was a young fellow named Bliss
Whose sex life was strangely amiss,
For even with Venus
His recalcitrant penis
Would never do better than t
                              h
                                i
                                  s

Anon., limerick (19th century)

But whilst her busy hand would guide that part
Which should convey my soul up to her heart,
In liquid raptures I dissolve all o'er,
Melt into sperm, and spend at every pore.
A touch from any part of her had done't:
Her hand, her foot, her very look's a cunt.

John Wilmot, Earl of Rochester, 'The Imperfect Enjoyment'
(1680)

He: You wanna quickie?
She: As opposed to what?

Anon.

It's the morning after the honeymoon, and the
wife says, 'You know, you're really a lousy lover.'
To which the husband replies, 'How can you tell
after only thirty seconds?'

Getting **DIRTY**

I can remember when the air was clean and sex was dirty.

George Burns

My psychiatrist asked me if I thought sex was dirty and I said 'It is if you're doing it right.'

Woody Allen, in Take the Money and Run *(1969)*

There's nothing inherently dirty about sex, but if you try real hard and use your imagination you can overcome that.

Lewis Grizzard

Sex is not some sort of pristine, reverent ritual. You want reverent and pristine, go to church.

Cynthia Heimel, Sex Tips for Girls *(1983)*

Women should be obscene and not heard.

John Lennon

I thank God I was raised Catholic, so sex will always be dirty.

John Waters

A Complete and Utter Pervert writes:

In libertinage, nothing is frightful, because everything libertinage suggests is also a natural inspiration; the most extraordinary, the most bizarre acts, those which most arrantly seem to conflict with every law, every human institution ... even those that are not frightful, and there is not one amongst them all that cannot be demonstrated within the boundaries of nature.

Marquis de Sade, *Philosophy of the Boudoir* (1795)

L'amour fait proprement est toujours sale.
(Love well done is always dirty.)

Anon.

Come on **DOWN**

Oral Sex

Oral sex: the taste of things to come.

Anon.

Cunnilingus is next to godliness.

Kali Nichta

Good girls get fat, bad girls get eaten.

Bumper sticker

Q: Why is pubic hair like parsley?
A: You push it to the side before you start eating.

Anon.

A Poet writes:

I'll be a park, and thou shalt be my deer;
Feed where thou wilt, on mountain or in dale:
Graze on my lips; and if those hills be dry,
Stray lower, where the pleasant fountains lie.

William Shakespeare, 'Venus and Adonis' (1593)

LET HIM WHO PUTS SEMEN IN THE MOUTH DO PENANCE
FOR SEVEN YEARS, FOR THIS IS THE WORST EVIL.

THEODORE OF TARSUS (7TH CENTURY)

Q: At the exact same time, there are two young men on opposite sides of the Earth: one is walking a tightrope between two skyscrapers, the other is getting a blow job from an 85-year-old woman. They are each thinking the same thing. What are they both thinking?

A: Don't look down!

Anon

Speaking of good taste …

She would blow him while he kneeled straddling her face … and then show him his pale semen inside her mouth, displayed on her arched tongue like a little Tachiste masterpiece before she swallowed it or disgorged it back onto his still-firm prick.

John Updike, Seek My Face (2003)

Q. What's the difference between love, true love and showing off?

A. Spitting, swallowing and gargling.

Anon.

If you're not into oral sex, keep your mouth shut!

Helmet sticker

If God had wanted people to give blow jobs, he wouldn't have given them teeth.

Anon.

Bruce and Bazza are herding roos in the Outback when suddenly a snake rears up and bites Bruce on the percy.

'Cripes, mate, that looks bad,' says Bazza, 'I'd better ride over to the station and radio the doc.'

An hour later he's on the radio, talking to the doc, who's asking him what kind of snake it was.

'Big green bastard with yellow stripes,' says Bazza.

'Dear me. Well, there's only one way to save your friend's life, and that's to suck out the venom.'

An hour later Bazza's back with his mate, whose lips are turning black.

'What's the doc say?' croaks Bruce.

'Sorry, mate. Doc says you'll be dead by sundown.'

Honey Mackintosh ... true to her Scottish roots ... sucked away like she was the last person left on earth to play the bagpipes on Robbie Burns' birthday.

Alan Parker, The Sucker's Kiss *(2003)*

You know the worst thing about oral sex? The view.

Maureen Lipman

Q: What's the difference between an airship and 365 blow jobs?
A: One's a Goodyear, but the other's an excellent year.

Anon.

I regret to say that we of the FBI are powerless to act in cases of oral-genital intimacy, unless it has in some way obstructed interstate commerce.

J. Edgar Hoover, attributed

Oh cwikey!

Alleged reaction in 1986 by health minister Norman Fowler (then in charge of the government's AIDS campaign) when told by his civil servants about the number of people who practised oral sex

Q: Why does a bride smile when she walks up the aisle?
A: She knows she has given her last blow job.

Anon.

There was a young lady from Leith
Who would circumcise men with her teeth
It wasn't for fame,
Or love of the game
But to get at the cheese underneath.

Anon.

As for that topsy-turvy tangle known as soixante-neuf, personally I have always felt it to be madly confusing, like trying to pat your head and rub your stomach at the same time.

Helen Lawrenson, quoted in Esquire *(1977)*

This one actually happened at Harvard University in a biology class.

The Professor was discussing the high glucose levels found in semen. A young female freshman raised her hand and asked, 'If I understand, you're saying there is as much glucose in semen as in sugar?' 'That's correct,' responded the Professor, going on to add statistical info. Raising her hand again, the girl asked, 'Then why doesn't it taste sweet?'

After a stunned silence, the whole class burst out laughing, the poor girl's face turned bright red and as she realized exactly what she had inadvertently implied, she picked up her books without a word and walked out of class ... and never returned.

However, as she was going out of the door, the Professor's reply was classic. Totally straight-faced, he answered her question. 'It doesn't taste sweet because the taste-buds for sweetness are on the tip of your tongue and not the back of your throat.'

An Orang-Utang Playing the **VIOLIN**

Tips on Technique

See also Playing Preludes: Foreplay; Bad Sex.

The majority of husbands remind me of an orang-utang trying to play the violin.

Honoré de Balzac

SKILL MAKES LOVE VNENDING.

OVID, THE ART OF LOVE

If you have been married more than ten years, being good in bed means you don't steal the covers.

Brenda Davidson

Cornering is like bringing a woman to a climax.

Jackie Stewart, racing driver. Brrrrm. Hmmm.

Lame men copulate best.

Mimnermus, Greek poet (7th century BC). With the addition of 'mad men', this has become proverbial, in an obscure sort of way.

If you watch lizards and lions copulating, then you will see that in 200,000,000 years the male has not had a single new idea.

Robert Ardrey, The Hunting Hypothesis *(1976)*

A Philosopher writes:

It is so characteristic, that just when the mechanics of reproduction are so vastly improved, there are fewer and fewer people who know how the music should be played.

Ludwig Wittgenstein

He: Shall we try a different position tonight?
She: OK. You stand by the ironing board while I sit on the sofa and fart.

Anon.

If I were asked for a one-line answer to the question 'What makes a woman good in bed?' I would say, 'A man who is good in bed.'

Bob Guccione, publisher of Penthouse *magazine*

Of Mrs Wallis Simpson's charm for the apparently poorly endowed Edward VIII:

She could make a matchstick seem like a Havana cigar.

Anon. It was said that Mrs Simpson had learnt the 'Chinese clutch' in Shanghai.

It's not how you fish, it's how you wiggle your worm.

Anon.

Too much of a good thing is wonderful!

Mae West

If there is reincarnation, I'd like to come back as Warren Beatty's fingertips.

Woody Allen

In Tantra, it is said that when your pinkie is in her anus, the next finger and middle finger in her yoni, and your thumb on her clitoris, you are holding one of the mysteries of the universe in your hand [… but apparently missing a finger. Ed.].

Anon.

Working **OUT**

Sexual Gymnastics

Sex is a body-contact sport. It is safe to watch but more fun to play.

Thomas Szasz

For the more agile there is this prohibition:

THOU SHALT NOT PRACTISE MASTURBATION EITHER WITH HAND OR WITH FOOT.

TALMUD.

I've tried several varieties of sex. The conventional position makes me claustrophobic and the others give me a stiff neck or lockjaw.

Tallulah Bankhead

I once knew a woman who offered her honour
So I honoured her offer
And all night long I was on her and off her.

Anon.

Remember, if you smoke after sex you're doing it too fast.

Woody Allen

There once was a man from Bel Air,
Who was doing his girl on the stair.
When the banister broke,
He doubled his stroke,
And finished her off in mid-air.

Anon.

Sex on television can't hurt you unless you fall off.

Anon.

I think there are two areas where new ideas are terribly dangerous: economics and sex. By and large, it's all been tried, and if it's really new, it's probably illegal or dangerous …

Felix G. Rohatyn

Orgasms
SCHMORGASMS

But did thee feel the earth move?

Ernest Hemingway, For Whom the Bell Tolls *(1940)*

Speaking of the earth moving …

I was in San Francisco when the great earthquake struck, but we were kinda busy in the bedroom and we didn't notice what was going on outside.

John Barrymore

On D.H. Lawrence's description of a female orgasm in *Lady Chatterley's Lover* (1928):

An enema under the influence of Ecstasy would probably feel much like this.

Germaine Greer, in the Independent on Sunday, *3 June 1990*

In the case of some women, orgasms take quite a bit of time. Before signing on with such a partner, make sure you are willing to lay aside, say, the month of June, with sandwiches having to be brought in.

Bruce Jay Friedman, 'Sex and the Lonely Guy' (1977)

All I got for Christmas was a sweater ... I would have preferred a screamer or a moaner.

Anon.

A chicken and an egg are lying in bed. The chicken is smoking a cigarette with a satisfied smile on its face and the egg is frowning and looking put out. The egg mutters to no one in particular, 'Well, I guess we answered *that* question.'

Anon.

COMING TOGETHER

To go together is blessed, to come together is divine.

Anon.

'Don't people often come off together?' she asked with naïve curiosity.

'A good many of them never. You can see by the raw look of them.'

D.H. Lawrence, Lady Chatterley's Lover *(1928)*

Most men think Mutual Orgasm is the name of an insurance company.

Anon.

Is there a way to accept the concept of the female orgasm and still command the respect of your foreign-auto mechanic?

Bruce Feirstein, Real Men Don't Eat Quiche *(1982)*

Q: How do you know when a female yuppie achieves orgasm?
A: She drops her briefcase.

Anon.

He: Why don't you tell me when you have an orgasm?
She: I would, but you're never there.

Anon.

How alike are the groans of love to those of the dying.

Malcolm Lowry, Under the Volcano *(1947)*

Isn't it interesting how the sounds are the same for an awful nightmare and great sex?

Line from TV show The Golden Girls

One of the principle differences between a woman and volcano is that a volcano doesn't fake eruptions.

Tim Dedopulos

A Doctor writes:

WHEN A WOMAN REACHES THE VERY GOAL OF
APHRODITE'S ACTION, SHE INSTINCTIVELY GASPS WITH
A BVRNING DELIGHT AND HER GASP RISES QUICKLY TO
THE LIPS WITH A LOVE-BREATH, AND THERE IT MEETS
A LOST KISS, WANDERING ABOUT AND LOOKING FOR
A WAY DOWN. THIS KISS MINGLES WITH THE LOVE-
BREATH AND RETURNS WITH IT TO STRIKE THE HEART.
THE HEART THEN IS KISSED, CONFUSED, THROBBING.
ACHILLES TATIUS, LEUCIPPE AND CLEITOPHON (5TH CENTURY)

The only thing wrong with being an atheist is that
there's nobody to talk to during an orgasm.
Anon.

'Mommy mommy, what's an orgasm?'
'I don't know, ask your father.'
Anon.

Q: What's the difference between a Catholic wife
and a Jewish wife?
A: A Catholic wife has real orgasms and fake
jewellery.
Anon.

To her French lover:

Now I know what I've been faking all these years.
Judy Benjamin (Goldie Hawn), in Private Benjamin *(1980)*

There was a young lady of Fakenham
Who was often suspected of fakin' 'em.
But with groans and loud sighs
And hyena-like cries –
Her joys? There was no mistakin' 'em.

Anon.

Party Guest: I finally had an orgasm and my
doctor told me it was the wrong kind.

Line from Manhattan *(1979), screenplay by Woody Allen and
Marshall Brickman*

*Woman in restaurant to Waitress (Sally having just
faked a noisy orgasm):* I'll have whatever she's
having.

Line from When Harry Met Sally *(1989), screenplay by Nora
Ephron*

There was a young plumber of Leigh
Who was plumbing a girl by the sea.
She said, 'Stop your plumbing,
There's somebody coming!'
Said the plumber, still plumbing,
'It's me.'

Anon.

Bad **SEX**

See also Playing Preludes: Foreplay; Tips on Technique.

I'm a terrible lover. I've actually given a woman an anti-climax.

Scott Roeben

I blame my mother for my poor sex life. All she told me was, 'The man goes on top and the woman underneath.' For three years my husband and I slept on bunk beds.

Joan Rivers

My girlfriend always laughs during sex – no matter what she's reading.

Steve Jobs

No sex is better than bad sex.

Germaine Greer

They each cling to opposite sides of the mattress, well away from the vast lagoon of semen in the centre of the bed, a thick coldness which will still be damp when Paul awakes the next morning.

Rod Liddle, Too Beautiful For You *(2003)*

WHAM, BAM, THANK YOU, MA'AM

I know I must be really good in bed, 'cause women always ask me if there's any possible way I could make it last longer.

Bill Hewins

At Oxford the select preacher, one evening service, speaking of venery, said, 'And let me implore you, my young friends, not to imperil your immortal souls upon a pleasure which, so I am credibly informed, lasts less than one and three-quarter minutes.'

T.E. Lawrence, The Mint *(1955)*

One night I made love from one o'clock to five past two. It was the time they put the clocks forward.

Gary Shandling

The thing that takes the least amount of time and causes the most amount of trouble is sex.

John Barrymore

We were fast and furious: I was fast and she was furious.

Max Kauffman

Slowly, but very deliberately, the brooding edifice of seduction, creaking and incongruous, came into being, a vast Heath Robinson mechanism, dually controlled by them and lumbering gloomily down vistas of triteness. With a sort of heavy-fisted dexterity the mutually adapted emotions of each of them became synchronized, until the unavoidable anti-climax was at hand.

Anthony Powell, The Afternoon Men *(1931)*

His penis was prodding her leg and she took it in her hand like the snout of a dog.

Tama Janowitz, Peyton Amberg *(2003)*

Housework is like bad sex. Every time I do it I swear I will never do it again. Until the next time company comes.

Marilyn Sokol

There is nothing so overrated as a bad fuck. There is nothing so underrated as a good shit.

Swami Chaitanya

There's nothing better than good sex. But bad sex? A peanut butter and jelly sandwich is better than bad sex.

Billy Joel

THE BAD SEX AWARDS

This annual prize is awarded by *The Literary Review* (London), not for descriptions of bad sex, but for bad descriptions of sex found in novels published that year. Here are a few short-listed contenders and winners:

He pulled the faded quilt from the bed and opened the sheets and she laid herself down and watched him take off his boots and socks and then his jeans and shorts. And he felt no shame nor saw any in her, for why should they feel shame at what was not of their making but of some deeper force that stormed not just their bodies but their souls and knew naught of shame nor of any such construct?

Nicholas Evans, The Horse Whisperer *(1996). Later, '. . . he saw Annie open herself before him and felt the soft collision of their flesh'.*

Meanwhile her ears were filled with the sound of a soft but frantic gasping and it was some time before she identified it as her own … 'This is so wonderful I feel I might disintegrate…'

Sebastian Faulks, Charlotte Gray *(1998). Faulks failed to turn up to collect his first prize (a bunch of cigars), but TV gardener Alan Titchmarsh received his runner-up prize for his first novel,* Mr MacGregor, *announcing, 'In the face of stiff opposition I'm glad I came.' Also short-listed in 1998 was US special prosecutor Kenneth Starr for his report on the Monica Lewinsky affair.*

It is time, time … Now. Yes. She is so small and compact and yet she has all the necessary features … Shall I compare thee to a Sony Walkman, thou art more compact and more – She is his own Toshiba, his dinky little JVC, his sweet Aiwa … Aiwa, aiwa aiwa aiwa aiwa aiwa aiwa aiwa aiwa aiwaaaaaaaaahhhhhhhhh …

Sean Thomas, Kissing England *(2000). Collecting his award (having beaten heavyweight contenders such as John Updike), Mr Thomas said, 'It's an enormous honour and I'm gratified … I think mine was by far the most outrageous passage.'*

Her hand is moving away from my knee and heading north. Heading unnervingly and with a steely will towards the pole. And, like Sir Ranulph Fiennes, Pamela will not easily be discouraged. I try twitching, and then shaking my leg, but to no avail. At last, disastrously, I try squeezing her hand painfully between my bony thighs, but this only serves to inflame her ardour the more. Ever northward moves her hand, while she smiles languorously at my right ear. And when she reaches the north pole, I think in wonder and terror ... she will surely want to pitch her tent.

Christopher Hart, Rescue Me *(2001) – another winner*

Weirdly, he was clad in pin-stripes at the same time as being naked. Pin-stripes were erotic, the uniform of fathers, two-dimensional fathers. Even Mr Hughes's penis had a seductive pin-striped foreskin.

Wendy Perriam, Tread Softly *(2002). It was third time lucky for Ms Perriam, who won in 2002 after being short-listed in the previous two years.*

'What's that?' you ask. You see a designer pussy. Hair razored and ordered in the shape of a swastika. The Aryan denominator ...

She sandwiches your nozzle between her tits, massaging it with a slow rhythm. A trailer to bookmark the events ahead. For now she has taken you in her lovely mouth. Your palms are holding her neck and thumbs are at her ears regulating the speed of her head as she swallows and then sucks up your machinery.

She is topping up your engine oil for the cross-country coming up. Your RPM is hitting a new high ...

She picks up a Bugatti's momentum. You want her more at a Volkswagen's steady trot. Squeeze the maximum mileage out of your gallon of gas. But she's eating up the road with all cylinders blazing ...

Aniruddha Bahal, Bunker 13 (2003)

As a lover, I'm about as impressive as a magician on the radio.

Scott Roeben

Three women were talking about their love lives.

  The first said, 'My husband is like a Rolls-Royce, smooth and sophisticated.'

  The second said, 'Mine is like a Porsche, fast and powerful.'

  The third said, 'Mine is like an old Chevy. It needs a hand start and I have to jump on while it's still going.'

Anon.

Alcohol is like love: the first kiss is magic, the second is intimate, the third is routine. After that you just take the girl's clothes off.

Raymond Chandler

If it's true that men only prefer watching football to having sex because football lasts longer, then the answer lies in their own hands.

Mary Riddell, in New Statesman, *1997*

Rough **STUFF**

If sex doesn't scare the cat, you're not doing it right.

Anon.

WHAT THEY LOVE TO YIELD THEY WOULD OFTEN RATHER HAVE STOLEN. ROUGH SEDUCTION DELIGHTS THEM, THE BOLDNESS OF NEAR RAPE IS A COMPLIMENT.
OVID, THE ART OF LOVE

You know women as well as I do. They are only willing when you compel them, but after that they're as enthusiastic as you are.

Jean Giraudoux, Tiger at the Gates *(1935)*

My husband's German. Every night I get dressed up as Poland and he invades me.

Bette Midler

A lover's pinch that hurts and is desired

William Shakespeare, *Antony and Cleopatra* (1606)

The Duke returned from the wars today and did pleasure me in his top-boots.

Sarah, Duchess of Marlborough (1660–1744)

You have to accept the fact that part of the sizzle of sex comes from the danger of sex. You can be overpowered.

Camille Paglia, Sex, Art and American Culture *(1992)*

WPC Sadie Stick
Won't you hit me with
your big black stick ...

Ian Drury

The Web is a dominatrix. Everywhere I turn, I see little buttons ordering me to Submit.

Nytwind

Tie Me Up, Tie Me **DOWN**

The uncertain and frenetic nature of modern life has led to the increasing popularity of mild bondage. When you're tied to the bed, at least you know where you're going to be for the next few minutes …

P.J. O'Rourke, Modern Manners *(1983)*

Bondage:

… the modern metropolitan equivalent of the camping weekend – plenty of straps and guy-ropes and hours of discomfort at the end of which you are soaking wet and sobbing quietly into a rubber sheet.

Rowena Raunchbitch, 'Torrid Sex Tips for Red-Hot Lovers', in the Rockall Times, *22 July 2002*

You don't appreciate a lot of stuff in school until you get older. Little things like being spanked every day by a middle-aged woman: Stuff you pay good money for in later life.

Emo Philips

I loved the Guides, that was where I learned to tie knots.

Lindi St Clair, professional dominatrix, quoted in The Independent, *1 July 1992*

An Expert writes:

Whoever allows himself to be whipped, deserves to be whipped.

Ritter Leopold von Sacher-Masoch, *Venus in Furs* (1870)

I had to give up masochism – I was enjoying it too much.

Mel Calman, Dr Calman's Dictionary of Psychoanalysis *(1979)*

I ache for the touch of your lips dear,
But much more for the touch of your whips dear,
You can raise welts
Like nobody else
As we dance to the Masochism Tango.

Tom Lehrer, 'The Masochism Tango' (1959)

I'm all for bringing back the birch, but only between consenting adults.

Gore Vidal, TV interview with David Frost, 1966

The Marquis de Sade and Genet
Are most highly thought of today,
But torture and treachery
Are not my sort of lechery,
So I've given my copies away.

W.H. Auden, in the New York Review of Books, *1966*

It's been so long since I made love, I can't even remember who gets tied up.

Joan Rivers

Some mornings, it's just not worth chewing through the leather straps.

Emo Philips

I love castigation mightily, I was so us'd to't at Westminster School that I could never leave it off since.

Thomas Shadwell, *The Virtuoso* (1676)

Ménages-à-Trois, Quatre, **CINQ** ...

Home is heaven and orgies are vile
But you need an orgy, once in a while.
Ogden Nash, '99.44100% Sweet Home' (1947)

Sex between a man and a woman can be
wonderful – provided you get between the right
man and the right woman.
Woody Allen

Group sex:
2 play 3 play 4play.
Anon. text message

Q: What's the definition of an orgy?
A: A party where everybody comes.
Anon.

I believe that sex is a beautiful thing between two
people. Between five, it's fantastic.
Woody Allen

Two is company. Three is fifty bucks.
Joan Rivers

If God had meant us to have group sex, he'd have given us more organs.

Malcolm Bradbury, 'A Very Hospitable Person', in Who Do You Think You Are? *(1976)*

On refusing his second invitation to an orgy, having accepted the first:

Once – a philosopher. Twice – a pervert.

Voltaire

The closest I ever came to a ménage-à-trois was when I dated a schizophrenic.

Rita Rudner

An orgy looks particularly alluring seen through the mists of righteous indignation.

Malcolm Muggeridge The Most of Malcolm Muggeridge, *'Dolce Vita in a Cold Climate' (1966)*

You get a better class of person at orgies, because people have to keep in trim more. There is an awful lot of going round holding in your stomach, you know. Everybody is very polite to each other. The conversation isn't very good, but you can't have everything.

Gore Vidal, interviewed on Russell Harty Plus *(1972)*

Unnatural Acts and Hidden **BYWAYS**

Kinky is using a feather. Perverted is using the whole chicken.

Anon. (also attributed to Elmore Leonard and to Roman Polanski, with the feather being 'erotic' and the chicken being 'kinky')

There is no norm in sex. Norm is the name of a guy who lives in Brooklyn.

Dr Alex Comfort, in Medical World News, *November 1974*

Sex is natural, but not if it's done right.

Anon.

The only unnatural sex act is one which you cannot perform.

Alfred Kinsey

If sex is such a natural phenomenon, how come there are so many books on how to do it?

Bette Midler

When choosing between two evils, I always try to choose the one I haven't tried before.

Mae West, Klondike Annie *(1936)*

Chastity: The most unnatural of the sexual perversions.

Aldous Huxley

Asked why he had come to America:

In pursuit of my life-long quest for naked women in wet mackintoshes.

Dylan Thomas

Of course, Salvador Dali seduced many ladies, particularly American heiresses; but those seductions usually entailed stripping them naked in his apartment, frying a couple of eggs, putting them on the woman's shoulders, and without a word showing them the door.

Luis Buñuel, Conversations with Buñuel *(1985)*

My classmates would copulate with anything that moved, but I never saw any reason to limit myself.

Emo Philips

Lonely bachelor David X was convicted yesterday of making love to a lamp-post. X, 57, was so desperate for sex he pulled his trousers and pants down by his ankles, wrapped his arms around the 30-ft pole and rubbed himself up and down.

The *Sun*

NERO SO PROSTITVTED HIS OWN CHASTITY, THAT AFTER DEFILING ALMOST EVERY PART OF HIS BODY, HE AT LAST DEVISED A KIND OF GAME IN WHICH, COVERED WITH THE SKIN OF SOME WILD ANIMAL, HE WAS LET LOOSE FROM A CAGE AND ATTACKED THE PRIVATE PARTS OF MEN AND WOMEN, WHO WERE BOVND TO STAKES...

SUETONIUS, LIVES OF THE TWELVE CAESARS (C.AD 100)

My girlfiend said to me in bed last night, 'You're a pervert.' I said, 'That's a big word for a girl of nine.'

Emo Philips

INCEST is Best

Vice is nice, but incest is best.

Graffito

Incest – a game the whole family can play.

Graffito

Oedipus, Schmoedipus, he loves his mother.

Anon.

My mother was like a sister to me, only we didn't have sex quite so often.

Emo Philips

What's wrong with a little incest? It's both handy and cheap.

James Agate

WHAT THE GOOD BOOK SAYS   4

THE NAKEDNESS OF THY SISTER . . . THOU SHALT NOT UNCOVER. THE NAKEDNESS OF THY SON'S DAUGHTER, OR OF THY DAUGHTER'S DAUGHTER, EVEN THEIR NAKEDNESS THOU SHALT NOT UNCOVER.
LEVITICUS 18:7–9

A Complete and Utter Pervert writes:

There is nothing more exquisite than carnal relations within the family.

Marquis de Sade *Philosophy in the Boudoir* (1795)

She said he proposed something on their wedding night that even her own brother wouldn't have suggested.

James Thurber

TALES FROM THE NET 3

A hillbilly couple from wildest Kentucky are on their honeymoon at the local motel. On the first night Mary-Lou turns to Seth and says, 'Hey, Seth, you go on and be gentle with me, cos I's a virgin.'

Surprised at this turn of events, Seth runs out to the phone booth and calls his father.

'I dunno what to do, pop, she says she's a virgin.'

His father sucks in a breath between his two remaining teeth and says, 'I'll tell you what to do, son, you come straight on home, d'y'hear? If she ain't good enough for her own family she sure ain't good enough for ours.'

Necrophilia

Dead Boring

Buggery is boring.
Incest is relatively boring.
Necrophilia is dead boring.
Graffito

There once was a man called Dave
Who kept a dead whore in a cave
He said, 'I admit
I'm a bit of a shit
But think of the money I save.'
Anon.

**... eating Sushi is like going down
on a corpse.**

Chris Paling, Newton's Swing *(2000)*

A RAVE FROM THE GRAVE

I met my love in the graveyard
I did her before we were wed
I laid her on top of the tombstone
We did it to cheer up the dead.

Brendan Behan, attributed

A widow whose singular vice
Was to keep her late husband on ice
Said, 'It's been hard since I lost him-
I'll never defrost him!
Cold comfort, but cheap at the price.'

Anon.

Anal **SEX**

Sodomy by Any Other Name Would Sound as Sweet

If you think sex is a pain in the ass, try a different position.

Anon.

... he leads me to the table and with a master-hand lays my head down on the edge of it, and, with the other canting up my petticoats and shift, bares my naked posteriours to his blind and furious guide; it forces its way between them, and I feeling pretty sensibly that it was not going by the right door, and knocking desperately at the wrong one, I told him of it: – 'Pooh!' says he, 'my dear, any port in a storm.'

John Cleland, *Memoirs of a Lady of Pleasure*, better known as *Fanny Hill* (1748–9)

TAKE AWAY PROSTITVTES FROM THE WORLD, AND YOU WILL FILL IT WITH SODOMY.
ST THOMAS AQUINAS, OPUSCULA

Trembling she comes, and with as little flame,
As he for the dear part from whence he came,
But by the help of an assisting thumb
Squeezes his chitterling into her bum;
And if it prove a straight, well-sphincter'd arse,
Perhaps it rears a little his feeble tarse.

Charles Sackville, Earl of Dorset, *A Faithful Catalogue of the Most Eminent Ninnies* (mid-17th century)

It is impossible to obtain a conviction for sodomy from an English jury. Half of them don't believe that it can physically be done, and the other half are doing it.

Winston Churchill

I bet the people of Gomorrah felt like they got the short end of the stick. After all, they didn't get a perversion named after them.

Mike Miles

On his first experience of colonic irrigation:

I feel I lost my virginity that day in so many ways.

Ben Affleck

One day Superman is flying around and because it's the first day of spring he's feeling really really horny. As he flies around he spots with his telescopic Super Vision Wonderwoman lying on the roof-top of her apartment block sunbathing naked. 'Wowee,' thinks Superman. 'Because I have Super Powers I can be in and out of there so quick she won't even see me.' So down he flies and sows his Super Oats, and then flies off, all in the blinking of an eye.

Wonderwoman starts up with a stupefied look. 'What in tarnation was that?'

'I don't know,' says the Invisible Man, 'but my ass is killing me.'

Q: What's the difference between oral sex and anal sex?
A: Oral sex makes your day, but anal sex makes your hole weak.

Anon.

A Melon for
ECSTASY

Rude Food

A woman for duty, a boy for pleasure, but a melon for ecstasy.

Arab saying (allegedly)

I love my little cucumber
So long, so firm, so straight.
So sad, my little cucumber,
We cannot propagate.

Anon. (19th century)

'Come, Big Boy, come,' screamed the maddened piece of liver, that, in my own insanity, I bought one afternoon at a butcher shop and, believe it or not, violated behind a billboard on the way to a bar mitzvah lesson.

Philip Roth, Portnoy's Complaint *(1969)*

Sex is the liquid centre of the great Newberry Fruit of friendship.

Jilly Cooper, Super-Jilly

I remember my first sexual encounter because I kept the recipe.

Jeff Dahmer, cannibal and mass-murderer

Q: What food sucks 80 per cent of the sex drive from a woman?
A: The wedding cake.

Anon.

Q: Why is food better than men?
A: Because you don't have to wait an hour for seconds.

Anon.

How you like – Anh
My sweet corn, baby – Onh
Plenty buttah – Anh
Anh – make you crazy – Onh

Lyric from E. Annie Proux, Accordion Crimes *(1996)*

Some things can't be ravished. You can't ravish a tin of sardines.

D.H. Lawrence, Lady Chatterley's Lover *(1928). Not with those sharp edges, anyway …*

A Doctor writes:

Most homosexuals find their man-to-man sex unfulfilling so they masturbate a lot … Carrots and cucumbers are pressed into service … Sometimes the whole egg in the shell finds itself where it doesn't belong. Sausages, especially the milder varieties, are popular. The homosexual who prefers to use his penis must find an anus. Many look in the refrigerator. The most common masturbatory object for this purpose is a melon. Cantaloupes are usual, but where it is available, papaya is popular.

Dr David Reuben, Everything You Always Wanted to Know About Sex, But Were Afraid to Ask *(1969)*

Can you dance the quick fandango in the dance
hall of your heart,
Can you eat a rotten mango, make love until you
fart?

I.D. Crack

Sex is the Tabasco sauce which an adolescent
national palate sprinkles on every course in the
menu.

May Day Winn, Adam's Rib *(1931)*

A terrible misconception:

'Put it in your mouth,' he said. 'Yes, as you would
a delicious thing to eat.' I like to broaden my mind
when I can and I did as he suggested, swallowing
it up entirely and biting it off with a snap. As I did
so my eager fellow increased his swooning to the
point of fainting away, and I, feeling both
astonished by his rapture and disgusted by the
leathery thing filling up my mouth, spat out what I
had not eaten and gave it to one of my dogs. The
whore from Spitalfields had told me that men like
to be consumed in the mouth, but it seems to me
a reckless act, for the member must take some
time to grow again.

Jeanette Winterson, Sexing the Cherry *(1989)*

PIZZA BELLA

Sex is like pizza, even if it's done bad, it's still good.

Anon.

Or perhaps not …

She confiscated the zapper and slid my hand between her thighs. It was wet and warm down there, which was only to be expected, but she might just as well have deposited my hand on a pizza for all the effect it had. I actually found myself wondering if I would be able to tell a pizza and my wife apart by touch alone, and my uncertainty saddened me immeasurably.

Doris Dörrie, Where Do We Go From Here? *(2001)*

I've heard it said that sex is like pizza – even when it's bad, it's still good. I guess what I want to know is where I can call to get it delivered within 30 minutes.

Sean P. McAskill

The perfect lover is one who turns into a pizza at 4 a.m.

Charles Pierce

What's Sauce for the Goose is Sauce for the
GANDER

Bestiality Mostly

An Argentine gaucho named Bruno
Once said, 'There is one thing I do know:
A woman is fine,
A sheep is divine,
But a llama is numero uno.'

Anon.

I think people should be free to engage in any
sexual practices they choose. They should draw
the line at goats though.

Elton John

The pilgrimage to Mecca is not complete without
having carnal knowledge of a camel.

Arab saying

I couldn't believe it the other day when I picked up a British newspaper and read that 82 per cent of men would rather sleep with a goat than me.

The Duchess of York, quoted in the Observer, *25 March 2001*

He was into animal husbandry – until they caught him at it.

Tom Lehrer, An Evening Wasted with Tom Lehrer *(1953)*

Play with each other. Play with yourselves. Just don't play with the squirrels, they bite.

Anon.

PANDA MATING FAILS; VETERINARIAN TAKES OVER

Newspaper headline

There was a young charmer called Sheba,
Whose pet was a wriggling amoeba.
This cute blob of jelly
Would lie on her belly
And blissfully murmur 'Ich liebe.'

Anon.

Q: What's the difference between a hamster and a turtle?
A: With a turtle you don't need duct tape.

Anon. [Me neither. Ed.]

Idiot! Don't throw him in prison, transfer him to the infantry.

Frederick the Great, on hearing that a cavalryman was on a charge for buggering his horse

When Dead-Eye Dick and Mexican Pete
Lived down by Dead Man's Creek,
They'd had no luck in the way of a fuck
For nigh on half a week.

Oh, a moose or two, and a caribou,
And a bison cow or so,
But for Dead-Eye Dick with his kingly prick
This fucking was mighty slow.

Anon., 'Eskimo Nell'

WHAT THE GOOD BOOK SAYS   5

IF A MAN LIE WITH A BEAST, HE SHALL SURELY BE PUT
TO DEATH; AND YE SHALL SLAY THE BEAST. AND IF A
WOMAN APPROACH UNTO ANY BEAST, AND LIE DOWN
THERETO THOU SHALT KILL THE WOMAN AND THE
BEAST; THEY SHALL SURELY BE PUT TO DEATH; THEIR
BLOOD SHALL BE UPON THEM.
LEVITICUS 20:15–16

Of I'm a Celebrity ... Get Me Out of Here!, featuring Jordan,
Johnny Rotten et al.

At least the contestants were eating the local fauna, rather than mating with it.

Mary Riddell, in the Observer, *8 February 2004*

There was a young woman called Myrtle
Who once was seduced by a turtle.
The result of this mate
Was five crabs and a skate,
Thus proving the turtle was fertile.

Anon.

NO ACCOUNTING FOR TASTES

When a woman has tasted a dog, she will never want a man again.

Attributed to a 19th-century female servant

On the uses of lapdogs …

… none without thy notice should approach
The Seat of Joy, which thou hast leave to touch,
And with thy icy Nose presum'st to kiss,
Without Offence, the very Gates of Bliss.

Edward Ward, 'The Secret History of Clubs' (1709)

Frederick Hanley would like to have a Bible bound with bits of skin stripped off live from the cunts of a hundred little girls and yet he could not be persuaded to try the sensation of fucking a Muscovy Duck whilst its head was cut off.

Sir Richard Burton (the explorer), attributed

She would lie down on a sofa and separating her thighs would smear honey on and in the vulva. The flies thus attracted by the honey would tickle her until her sexual appetite was appeased

G. Herzog, Medical Jurisprudence *(1894)*

A man accused of having sex with a chicken told Nottingham Crown Court in October 1990 that he was checking to see if an egg was on the way. The prosecutor observed: 'That fails quite markedly to explain why he should have his trousers down around his buttocks.'

The Observer, *4 October 1992*

Yeah, I'm a nat'r'ist, babe,
I lak dem beavers, babe,
Dem steamin' beavers, babe,
Wet an furry fo ma –
Hot an pussy-purrin fo ma –
A-meeeeooowin fo ma, yeah,
Ma cock-a-doodle-doo, babe.

Rollin' Joe Haggart, 'Nature-Lover's Blues' *(c.1947)*

A case is related where a number of congenial souls amused themselves with fishes, by inserting the tail ends of the live fish into the vulva and then by pressing the head of the fish, would start it to squirming, thus tickling the vulva.

G. Herzog, Medical Jurisprudence *(1894)*

A vice most obscene and unsavoury
Holds the Bishop of Balham in slavery:
With maniacal howls
He rogers young owls
Which he keeps in an underground aviary.

Anon.

Mary had a little lamb. That's what you get for sleeping in a barn.

Anon.

EEYORE SHOULD BE SO LUCKY

The rites of the Good Goddess! Shrieking flutes excite the women's loins, wine and trumpet madden them, whirling and shrieking, rapt by Priapus. Then, then, their hearts are burning with lust, their voices stammer with it, their wine gushes in torrents down their soaking thighs. Their itching cannot bear delay: this is sheer Woman, shrieking and crying everywhere in the hall, 'It is time, let in the men' … And if no man can be found, they content themselves with an ass.

Juvenal, Satires

Hot **DOGS**

Animal-on-Animal Action

The rabbit has a charming
   face:
Its private life is a disgrace.
I really dare not name to
   you
The awful things that
   rabbits do.

Anon., 'The Rabbit' (c.1925)

The thoughts of a rabbit on sex,
Are seldom, if ever, complex.
For a rabbit in need
Is a rabbit in deed
And does just what a person expects.

Anon.

I like frogs because they get together in warm
moist places and sing about sex.

Anon.

'But what *is* the love-life of newts, if you boil it right down? Didn't you tell me once that they just waggled their tails at each other in the mating season?'

'Quite correct.'

'Well, all right if they like it. But it's not my idea of molten passion.'

P.G. Wodehouse, The Code of the Woosters *(1938)*

Among the porcupines, rape is unknown.

Gregory Clark

LETTER TO A PET THERAPIST

Quoted in Peter Neville, *Pet Sex* (1993)

Dear Mr Neville

We have regretted the day we bought our son a new bike for his birthday. His bright red racing bike has become an irresistible object of desire for Henry, our four-year-old black labrador. The bike is parked at night in our front hallway for security and Henry spends the evening trying to mount it from the front wheel angle or the rear. Come the morning or at any time when our son tries to take the bike out of the door, Henry must think that his lover is walking out on him because he tries desperately to mount it again and keep it in. More than once, son, bike and dog have ended up in an unholy heap by the front door. What on earth is going through our dog's mind?

Yours sincerely

Lesley and Alastair George

Asked why he wouldn't drink water:

Fish fuck in it.

W.C. Fields

Although humans tend to view sex as mainly a fun recreational activity sometimes resulting in death, in nature it is a far more serious matter.

Dave Barry

Approach a mule the way a porcupine makes love: Slow 'n keerful.

Anon.

A Syphilitic Philosopher writes:

Be not too free and easy; it doth belong
To dogs alone to screw the whole day long.

Friedrich Nietzsche, The Genealogy of Morals *(1899)*

Old sloths who hang down from twigs do it,
Though the effort is great,
Sweet guinea-pigs do it,
Buy a couple and wait.
The world admits bears in pits do it,
Even pekineses in the Ritz do it,
Let's do it, let's fall in love.

Cole Porter, 'Let's Fall in Love' *(1930)*

Sex, Lies and ...
Sex EDUCATION

My father told me all about the birds and the bees, the liar – I went steady with a woodpecker till I was twenty-one.

Bob Hope

To a five-year-old girl enquiring what a couple of dogs were doing:

The doggie in front has suddenly gone blind, and the other one has very kindly offered to push him all the way to St Dunstan's.

Noël Coward

I know so much about men because I went to night school.

Mae West

Conservatives say teaching sex education in the public schools will promote promiscuity. With our education system? If we promote promiscuity the same way we promote math or science, they've got nothing to worry about.

Beverly Mickins

The best sex education for kids is when Daddy pats Mommy on the fanny when he comes home from work.

William H. Masters [That's an American fanny. Ed.]

He said it was artificial respiration but now I find I'm to have his child.

Anthony Burgess, Inside Mr. Enderby *(1963)*

It's important to pay close attention in school – for years I thought that bears masturbated all winter.

Damon R. Milhem

A Vision in Pink writes:

A man will teach his wife what is needed to arouse his desires. And there is no reason for a woman to know any more than what her husband is prepared to teach her. If she gets married knowing far too much about what she wants and doesn't want then she will be ready to find fault with her husband.

Barbara Cartland

There's very little advice in men's magazines, because men think, 'I know what I'm doing. Just show me somebody naked.'

Jerry Seinfeld

A delighted incredulous bride
Remarked to the groom at her side,
I never could quite
Believe till tonight
Our anatomies would coincide.

Anon.

There was a young girl of Cape Cod
Who thought babies were fashioned by God;
But 'twas not the Almighty
Who hiked up her nightie,
But Roger the lodger, the sod!

Anon.

I bought my wife a sex manual but half the pages
were missing. We went straight from foreplay to
post-natal depression.

Bob Monkhouse

Contraception

Buy Me and Stop One

Learn from your parents' mistakes – use birth control.

Bumper sticker

Contraceptives should be used on every conceivable occasion.

Spike Milligan, The Last Goon Show of All *(1972)*

The best contraceptive is a glass of cold water: not before or after, but instead.

Anon. delegate at an international Planned Parenthood Conference

Apparently you can temporarily sterilize yourself by heating one's organs in boiling water.

Anon. British teenager

My best birth control now is just to leave the lights on.

Joan Rivers

A vasectomy means never having to say you're sorry.

Graffito

I want to tell you a terrific story about oral contraception. I asked this girl to sleep with me and she said, 'No.'

Woody Allen

Jane Fonda to teens: Use head to avoid pregnancy

Q: What do women and condoms have in common?
A: They both spend more time in your wallet than on your penis.

Anon.

Just saying 'no' prevents teenage pregnancy the way 'Have a nice day' cures chronic depression.

Faye Wattleton

I have no luck with women. I once went on a date and asked the woman if she'd brought any protection. She pulled a switchblade on me.

Scott Roeben

New coil inserted. Recall Edward II disembowelled at Berkeley Castle.

Sue Limb, Dulce Domum's Bad Housekeeping

RHYTHM AND BLUES:
CATHOLICS AND CONTRACEPTION

Q. What do you call people who use the rhythm method?
A. Parents.

Anon.

It is now quite lawful for a Catholic woman to avoid pregnancy by a resort to mathematics, though she is still forbidden to resort to physics or chemistry.

H.L. Mencken

I would not allow one of my babies to be adopted by a couple who practice contraception. People who use contraceptives do not understand the meaning of love.

Mother Teresa, in 1983

Protestant women may take the Pill.
Roman Catholic women must keep taking the *Tablet*.

Irene Thomas (The Tablet is a Roman Catholic newspaper.)

The pope does not know about American Catholics. He doesn't know how to gear down a Porsche, he can't work a cigarette machine, doesn't know about Bank Americard – doesn't know about any of your problems. And the big issue, contraception – he never makes it with anybody! He lives in a state of celibacy, and I respect him for this, but he cannot relate to a problem about it, then, if he is that far removed from it, man.

Lenny Bruce

Regarding the Pope's strictures against contraception:

He no play-da-game.
He no make-a-da rules!

Earl Butz

Every sperm is sacred,
Every sperm is great,
If a sperm is wasted,
God gets quite irate.

Monty Python, The
Meaning of Life *(1982)*

I took my time opening the orange and white packet, fumbling on purpose. Tasty Ticklers: peaches and cream flavour. When I tore the foil, a smell like tinned fruit cocktail escaped into the room. Tinned fruit, and Carnation. Sunday tea at my grandmother's. The condom itself smelt worse, like children's medicine mixed with powdered milk ...

Simon Armitage, Little Green Man *(2001)*

I was sued by a woman who claimed she became pregnant because she watched me on TV and I bent her contraceptive coil.

Uri Geller

Safe **SEX**

Condoms aren't completely safe. A friend of mine
was wearing one and got hit by a bus.

Bob Rubin

I practise safe sex
I use an airbag.

Garry Shandling

There is nothing safe about sex. There never
will be.

Norman Mailer, in the International Herald Tribune,
24 June 1992

Sex, like the city streets, would be risk-free only
in totalitarian regimes.

Camille Paglia, Sex, Art and American Culture *(1992)*

Practise safe sex: go fuck yourself.

Helmet sticker

A Pox Upon **IT**

The Clap and Worse

Sex is the invention of a very clever venereal disease.

David Cronenberg

Flies spread disease – keep yours zipped.

Anon.

I love you so much it hurts...
...when I pee.

Department of Health STD campaign, February 2004

It is unthinkable for a Frenchman to arrive at middle age without having syphilis and the Croix de la Légion d'Honneur.

André Gide

Before you take a girl to bed these days you have to have a medical discussion about the plague. So I don't bother much.

Jack Nicholson, quoted in the Independent, *27 February 1993*

For the first time in history, sex is more dangerous than the cigarette afterward.

Jay Leno

My message to the businessmen of this country when they go abroad on business is that there is one thing above all they can take with them to stop them catching AIDS, and that is the wife.

Edwina Currie, then a junior health minister, quoted in the Guardian, *13 February 1987. She herself had earlier been shagging the brains out of Norma Major's husband.*

Statistically … you have more chance of contracting Aids from a Catholic priest than from a prostitute.

Nina Lopez-Jones, spokeswoman for the English Collective of Prostitutes, quoted in the Independent on Sunday, *13 September 1992*

NEVER WITHHOLD HERPES INFECTION FROM LOVED ONE

Headline from the Albuquerque Journal, *26 December 1984*

Despite a lifetime of service to the cause of sexual liberation, I have never caught venereal disease, which makes me feel rather like an Arctic explorer who has never had frostbite.

Germaine Greer

These days, you fuck someone, your arm drops off.

Bette Midler, quoted in the Independent, *12 November 1988*

Life is a sexually transmitted disease and the mortality rate is one hundred per cent.

R.D. Laing

Don't mistake a date who's a looker, a shot of booze and my penis willin' with a date with a hooker, ooze and a shot of penicillin.

Anon.

Oh Valentine, since you came to me
You're always in my thoughts.
I'll never forget the night we met
And you gave me genital warts.

Department of Health STD campaign, February 2004

What more fiendish proof of cosmic irresponsibility than a Nature which, having invented sex as a way to mix genes, then permits to arise, amid all its perfumed and hypnotic inducements to mate, a tireless tribe of spirochaetes and viruses that torture and kill us for following orders?

John Updike, Self-Consciousness: Memoirs *(1989)*

Deprived of
DEPRAVITY

Not Getting Any

See also Abstinence (But Not Yet).

A terrible thing happened to me last night again –
nothing.

Phyllis Diller

I'd like to get married because I like the idea of a
man being required by law to sleep with me every
night.

Carrie Snow

Sex is like the air: it's not important unless you
aren't getting any.

Anon.

Knowing what I do now about women, if I could
just travel back in time to when I was 16 years old,
I bet I would have gotten laid by now.

Ed Smith

The last time I was inside a woman was when I visited the Statue of Liberty.

Woody Allen, Crimes and Misdemeanours *(1989)*

The only reason I would take up jogging is so that I could hear heavy breathing again.

Erma Bombeck

There's no shortage of pussy – it's just the delivery system that's messed up.

Dr Roy V. Schenk

Poets' Corner 7

On being asked whether he had any regrets:

Yes, I haven't had enough sex.

John Betjeman, interviewed on BBC TV, 1983

There was an old lady from Leicester,
And no man had ever caressed her,
And all day she'd wriggle
And giggle and jiggle,
As though seven devils possessed her.

Anon.

On being asked whether he was gay:

That's a bit like asking a man crawling across the Sahara whether he would prefer Perrier or Malvern Water.

Alan Bennett, quoted in the Observer, *12 June 1988*

On some of the Pacific islands there were so few women that the guys in the forces would start howling at the sight of two coconuts close together.

Bob Hope

If it wasn't for pick-pockets I'd have no sex life at all.

Rodney Dangerfield

Sex is hereditary. If your parents never had it, chances are you won't either.

Joseph Fischer

I've been on so many blind dates, I should get a free dog.

Wendy Liebman

A woman wakes up to find her drunken husband trying to stuff aspirins into her mouth.

'What the hell are you doing?' she yells.

'Don't you have a headache?' he says.

'No I do not.'

'Brilliant. Let's shag.'

To all virgins … thanks for nothin'.

Bumper sticker

They say if you have positive thoughts about something, it will happen. Well, I've been thinking positively about my neighbour's 19-year-old daughter, but so far, no luck. I think maybe my wife's negative thoughts are interfering.

Maurizio Mariotti

An egg is the unluckiest darn thing in all creation: it only gets laid once, it only gets eaten once, it takes ten minutes to get hard, it comes in a box with eleven other guys, and the only one who ever sits on its face is its mom.

Anon.

Of the late 1960s / early 1970s:

There we were in the middle of a sexual revolution wearing clothes that guaranteed we wouldn't get laid.

Denis Leary

Masturbation

Making Love to Your Best Friend

Nothing is better than sex.
Masturbation is better than nothing.
Therefore, masturbation is better than sex.

Anon.

Woman: You are the greatest lover I have ever known.
Allen: Well, I practise a lot on my own.

Woody Allen, Love and Death *(1975)*

Don't knock masturbation, it's sex with someone you love.

Woodie Allen, Annie Hall *(1977)*

If God had intended us not to masturbate, He would have made our arms shorter.

George Carlin

We have reason to believe that man first walked upright to free his hands for masturbation.

Lily Tomlin

The church's condemnation of masturbation (and of contraception) is based solely on the following passage:

AND ONAN KNEW THAT THE SEED SHOULD NOT BE HIS; AND IT CAME TO PASS, WHEN HE WENT IN UNTO HIS BROTHER'S WIFE, THAT HE SPILLED IT ON THE GROUND, LEST THAT HE SHOULD GIVE SEED TO HIS BROTHER. GENESIS 38:9. MANY CENTURIES LATER DOROTHY PARKER CALLED HER CANARY ONAN, BECAUSE HE WAS ALWAYS SPILLING HIS SEED ON THE GROUND.

The good thing about masturbation is that you don't have to get dressed up for it.

Truman Capote. The film director Milos Forman thought that its best point was that 'You don't have to talk afterwards.'

The trouble with my sex life is that it too often takes place with just one consenting adult.

Anon.

I'll come and make love to you at five o'clock. If I'm late, start without me.

Tallulah Bankhead

How lucky we are that we can reach our genitals instead of that spot on our back that itches.

Flash Rosenberg

Sex is like anything else; if you want it done right you have to do it yourself.

Anon.

As I fill out the job application and get to the part about 'Sex: F or M', I never know which to choose – I really like to 'F', but spend most of the time alone 'M'-ing.

Tony J. Podrasky

CONTRA-ONAN: THE BLIND LEADING THE BLIND

A Doctor writes:

Masturbation produces seminal weakness, impotence, dysury, tabes dorsalis, pulmonary consumption, dyspepsia, dimness of sight, vertigo, epilepsy, hypochondriasis, loss of memory, managlia, fatuity, and death.

Benjamin Rush, Medical Inquiries and Observations upon Diseases of the Mind *(1812)*

A Chief Scout writes:

It is called in our schools *'beastliness'*, and this is about the best name for it ... should it become a habit it quickly destroys both health and spirits; he becomes feeble in body and mind, and often ends in a lunatic asylum ... A large number of lunatics in our asylums have made themselves ill by indulging in this vice, although at one time they were sensible, cheery boys like any one of you.

Robert Baden-Powell, Scouting for Boys *(1908)*

Masturbation: the primary sexual activity of mankind. In the nineteenth century it was a disease; in the twentieth, it's a cure.

Thomas Szasz

I am sure sex with a woman is nice, but it's not as good as the real thing.

Charles Hawtree, quoted in a biography of the Carry On *star*

A woman occasionally is quite a serviceable substitute for masturbation.

Karl Kraus

When you wake up in the morning and you're
   feeling grand,
And you've such a funny feeling in your seminary
   gland,
And you haven't got a woman – what's the matter
   with your hand
As you revel in the joys of copulation.

Song popular with British troops in the Second World War, sung to the tune of 'John Peel'

What do you call a tall guy who can masturbate ten times in a single day ? No, it's not a joke, I really need to know, because I want to put it on my résumé.

Damon R. Milhem

The man who said 'A bird in the hand's worth two in the bush' has been putting his bird in the wrong bushes.

Anon.

One orgasm in the bush is worth two in the hand.

Robert Reisner

The top ten reasons why masturbation is better than sex:
10.
9.
8.
7.
6.
5.
4.
3.
2.
1.

Anon.

And we were poor too. Why, if I hadn't been born a boy, I'd have had nothing to play with.

Rodney Dangerfield

Sex is like a bridge game; if you don't have a good partner, you better have a good hand.

Charles Pierce

Double-Clicking Your **MOUSE**

Female Masturbation

If sex is so personal, why are we expected to share it with someone else?

Lily Tomlin

It [masturbation] is the bulwark of virginity.

Elizabeth I, thus scurrilously attributed by Mark Twain

Masturbation is the thinking woman's television.

Christopher Hampton, The Philanthropist *(1970)*

Do you mean you've never double-clicked your mouse?

Line from
American Pie *(1999)*

Sylvia, the fair, in the bloom of fifteen,
Felt an innocent warmth as she lay on the green;
She had heard of a pleasure, and something she guessed
By the towzing, and tumbling, and touching her breast.
John Dryden, 'Sylvia the Fair' (1699)

On the pros of self-pleasuring:

The clear advantage is that this chore can be quickly got out of the way without the need for third-party intervention, without the necessity to appear naked in front of a man and without the requirement to lower oneself reluctantly onto his hideously empurpled virile member.

Rowena Raunchbitch, 'Torrid Sex Tips for Red-Hot Lovers', in the Rockall Times, *26 August 2002*

Never Mind the
BZZZZCOCKS

Vibrators and Other
Consumer Durables

Why did God create men? Because
vibrators can't mow the lawn.

Madonna, in the film Snake Eyes, *aka*
Dangerous Game *(1993)*

Since most men can't keep it up for long enough
to fulfil woman's God-given – and soon to be
Constitutioned – right to orgasm, the vibrator can
take over while the man takes a leak.

Gore Vidal, in Rolling Stone *(1980)*

Womola, what's a vibwator? What do people use
it for?

*Norman Fowler, who as health minister in 1986 was in charge of
the government's AIDS campaign; he is said to have addressed this
query to Romola Christopherson, Head of Information at the
Department of Health*

If you use the electric vibrator near water, you will come and go at the same time.

Louise Sammon

Nymphomaniacal Alice
Used a dynamite stick for a phallus.
They found her vagina
In North Carolina
And her ass-hole in Buckingham Palace.

Anon.

For when cunts swell, and glow with strong desire,
'Tis only pricks can quench the lustful fire;
And when that's wanting, dildoes must supply
The place of pricks upon necessity.

Johannes Meursius, *The Delights of Venus* (17th century)

Come on, tell me,
Tell me, tell me, tell me,
Who's ever, who's ever, who's ever bin
Shagged in Tenby
By a big black rubber bendy …

The Valley Girls, 'A Girls' Nite Out in Wales' (1984)

I think the reason guys like women in leather outfits so much is because they have that *new car* smell.

George Fara

Sex experts are puzzling over the strange case of 'George' who fell in love with an Austin Metro and developed a close erotic relationship with the machine ... George, 20, came from a family who belonged to a strict religious sect. He was a shy student with little social life and no sexual involvement with women because this would have invoked disapproval from his parents. But his life changed when the family acquired an Austin Metro car ... George, confused but happy, began to masturbate inside the car, or crouching down behind it next to the exhaust pipe. He was excited by the exhaust pipe especially if the engine was running and it was emitting fumes.

The Independent, *7 December 1992*

There are a number of mechanical devices which increase sexual arousal, particularly in women. Chief among these is the Mercedes-Benz 380 SL convertible.

P.J. O'Rourke

Asked what he would be taking to the World Cup finals in France in 1998:

My soccer boots and an inflatable doll, because a month without a woman would be difficult.

Eric Deflandre, Belgian footballer

A fanatic gun-lover named Crust
Was perverse to the point of disgust.
His idea of a peach
Had a sixteen-inch breech
And a pearl-handled .44 bust.

Anon.

The night of Alfred's seventy-fifth birthday had found Chip alone at Tilton Ledge pursuing sexual congress with his red chaise-longue.

Jonathan Franzen, The Corrections *(2001)*

One witness told the commissioners that she had seen sexual intercourse taking place between two parked cars in front of her house.

The Press *(Atlantic City, New Jersey), 14 June 1979*

Call in the
PROFESSIONALS

Women: you can't live with them, you can't live without them. That's probably why you can rent one for the evening.

Jim Stark

REMOVE PROSTITVTES FROM HVMAN AFFAIRS AND YOU WILL POLLVTE ALL THINGS WITH LVST.

ST AUGUSTINE, DE ORDINE *(5TH CENTURY)*

If courtesans and strumpets were to be prosecuted with as much rigour as some silly people would have it, what locks or bars would be sufficient to preserve the honour of our wives and daughters?

Bernard Mandeville, *The Fable of the Bees* (1714, rev. 1723)

The best things in life are free ... Try explaining that to an angry prostitute.

Daniel Bokor

A country without bordellos is like a house without bathrooms.

Marlene Dietrich, Marlene Dietrich's ABC *(1962)*

Treat a whore like a lady and a lady like a whore

Wilson Mizner, US playwright (1876–1933)

So do not think of helpful whores
as aberrational blots;
I could not love you half so well
without my practice shots.

James Stewart Alexander Simmons, 'Cavalier Lyric'

Oh, my name is Diamond Lily,
I'm a whore in Piccadilly
And my father runs a brothel in the Strand,
My brother sells his arsehole
To the Guards at Windsor Castle,
We're the finest fucking family in the land.

Anon., 'Diamond Lily'

The big difference between sex for money and
sex for free is that sex for money costs less.

Brendan Francis

Sex is one of the most wholesome, beautiful and
natural experiences that money can buy.

Steve Martin

Prostitution gives her an opportunity to meet
people. It provides fresh air and wholesome
exercise, and it keeps her out of trouble.

Joseph Heller, Catch-22 (1961)

When a guy goes to a hooker, he's not paying her for sex, he's paying her to leave.

Anon.

Writing is a lot like sex. At first you do it because you like it. Then you find yourself doing it for a few close friends and people you like. But if you're any good at all ... you end up doing it for money.

Anon.

There was an old girl of Kilkenny,
Whose usual charge was a penny,
For half of that sum,
You might fondle her bum,
A source of amusement to many.

Anon.

In the wake of the Profumo–Christine Keeler affair, the future prime minister tutted:

There is something utterly nauseating about a system of society which pays a harlot 25 times as much as it pays the prime minister, 250 times as much as it pays its members of Parliament, and 500 times as much as it pays some of its ministers of religion.

Harold Wilson, speech in the House of Commons, June 1963

DIAL X FOR … PHONE SEX

I'm too shy to express my sexual needs except over the phone to people I don't know.

Garry Shandling

When a man talks dirty to a woman, it's sexual harassment. When a woman talks dirty to a man, it's $3.95 a minute.

Steven Wright

During sex my girlfriend always wants to talk to me. Just the other night she called me from a motel …

Rodney Dangerfield

If my business was legitimate, I would deduct a substantial percentage for depreciation of my body.

Xaviera Hollander, The Happy Hooker *(1972)*

In my day, we did it the proper way – £25 without extras, food and drink, and a choice of ladies. We knocked off £5 for old-age pensioners and we charged men half-price if they were past it, and just fancied watching.

Cynthia Paine, former madam, in the Guardian, *27 March 2004*

I'm not cheap, but I am on special this week.
Anon.

It is a silly question to ask a prostitute why she
does it …These are the highest-paid 'professional'
women in America.
Gail Sheehy, Hustling *(1971)*

TALES FROM THE NET   6

A koala picks up a prostitute in a bar and goes
back to her flat. After a night in which the
koala gives the girl some magnificent head,
the cute marsupial makes to leave. 'Hey,' says
the girl, 'you ain't paid me yet.' Just in case
the bear isn't au fait with the professional
niceties, she shows him the definition of
prostitute in the dictionary: 'prostitute, *n.* A
woman who sells sex for money.'

Without batting an eyelid, the koala flicks
through the dictionary to the letter K, and
points his paw: 'koala bear, *n.* A chubby
marsupial. Eats bush and leaves.'

[Eat your heart out, Lynne Truss.]

A notorious whore named Miss Hearst
In the weakness of men is well versed.
Reads a sign over the head
Of her well-rumpled bed:
'The customer always comes first.'

Anon.

A Canadian man pretending to be a police officer demanded free sex from an undercover police officer pretending to be a prostitute. Trevor Blair Roszell, 35, was fined around £370 in Edmonton's provincial court for impersonating a police officer. Detectives say he flashed police ID and asked for free sex – or at least a reduced rate.

Ananova

In love as in sport, the amateur status must be strictly maintained.

Robert Graves

Word to the wise for men: Although meant as a compliment 'You make love like a professional!' isn't always received as such.

Derek Cockram

'How was your honeymoon?'

'Fine, except in the morning I made the mistake of handing my wife a $100 bill.'

'Oops.'

'No, it was all right. She gave me $50 change.'

Anon.

Ms St Clair claims she loves her work. 'I'm an extrovert nymphomaniac,' she says. 'It's perfect for me.' Her pleasures are 'sleeping, eating, counting money and sex – in that order'... She insists that she has turned down scores of offers of marriage – 'Why buy a book when you can join a library?'

Lindi St Clair, quoted in the Independent, 25 April 1992

Ann Landers says that you are addicted to sex if you have sex more than three times a day, and that you should seek professional help. I have news for Ann Landers: The only way I am going to get sex three times a day is if I seek professional help.

Jay Leno

Q: How do you make a hormone?
A: Don't pay her.

Anon.

The Actor and the Streetwalker ... the two oldest professions in the world – ruined by amateurs.

Alexander Woollcott, Shouts and Murmurs *(1922)*

Sex is like art. Most of it is pretty bad, and the good stuff is out of your price range.

Scott Roeben

What do you call men who take money from prostitutes? Magistrates.

Slogan of the English Collective of Prostitutes, quoted in the Independent, *11 November 1992*

Pornucopia

See also Giving the Judge an Erection: Obscenity and Censorship.

If Glenda Jackson can show her boobs and call it art, why can't I?

Samantha Fox, interview in The Times, *5 December 1992*

The difference between pornography and erotica is lighting.

Gloria Leonard

Pornography is in the groin of the beholder.

Anon.

Obscenity is what happens to shock some elderly and ignorant magistrate.

Bertrand Russell

Pornography is supposed to arouse sexual desires. If pornography is a crime, when will they arrest makers of perfume?

Richard Fleischer

I would read *Playboy* magazine more often, but my glasses keep steaming over.

George Burns

Pornography is literature designed to be read with one hand.

Angela Lambert, in the Independent on Sunday, *18 February 1990*

Filthy literature is a great moral wrecker. It is creating criminals faster than jails can be built.

J. Edgar Hoover, speech, 1951

A dirty book is rarely dusty.

Proverb

It's red hot, mate. I hate to think of this sort of book getting into the wrong hands. As soon as I've finished this, I shall recommend they ban it.

Tony Hancock, Hancock's Half-Hour, *26 February 1960*

No one ever died from an overdose of pornography.

William Margold

Fill in the blank with the best word or phrase:
He awoke with a start when two —— slipped
naked into his bed.
A: *Federal judges*
B: *Militant feminists*
C: *Burglars*
D: *Teenage girls*

Seeing her 42-inch ——, I grew excited.
A: *Husband*
B: *Bowling trophy*
C: *Bust*
D: *Heels*
Alphonse Simonaitis, 'Porno Writer's Aptitude Test'

Sex is more exciting on the screen and between
the pages than between the sheets.
Andy Warhol, From A to B and Back Again (1975)

What is wrong with pornography is that it is a
successful attempt to sell sex for more than it is
worth.
Quentin Crisp

Pornography is rather like trying to find out about
a Beethoven symphony by having somebody tell
you about it and perhaps hum a few bars.
Robertson Davies, 'The Table Talk of Robertson Davies' (1990)

Those Romans who perpetrated the rape of the Sabines, for example, did not work themselves up for the deed by screening *Debbie Does Dallas,* and the monkish types who burned a million or so witches in the Middle Ages had almost certainly not come across *Boobs and Buns* or related periodicals.

Barbara Ehrenreich, 'Our Neighbourhood Porn Committee' (1986)

Its avowed purpose is to excite sexual desire, which, I should have thought, is unnecessary in the case of the young, inconvenient in the case of the middle aged, and unseemly in the old.

Malcolm Muggeridge, Tread Softly For You Tread On My Jokes *(1966)*

It'll be a sad day for sexual liberation when the pornography addict has to settle for the real thing.

Brendan Francis

Proposed letter to *The Times*:

Dear Sir,

I hope I am not being a prude, but I feel compelled to lodge a protest against the ever-increasing flood of obscenity in dreams. Many of my friends have been as shocked and sickened as myself by the filth that is poured out nightly as soon as our eyes are closed. It is certainly not my idea of 'home entertainment' …

Kenneth Tynan, The Sound of Two Hands Clapping *(1975)*

In adolescence, pornography is a substitute for sex, whereas in adulthood, sex is a substitute for pornography.

Edmund White

My reaction to porn films is as follows: After the first ten minutes, I want to go home and screw. After the first twenty minutes, I never want to screw again as long as I live.

Erica Jong

When I was your age, when there wasn't any Internet, I had to walk barefoot in the snow to the corner shop and sneak my porn home in a brown paper bag the way God intended.

Anon.

Something for the Ladies

Frà Bartolommeo did a nude St Sebastian with very good flesh colouring, of sweet aspect and great personal beauty ... It is said that while this figure was on exhibition in the church the friars found out by the confessional that women had sinned in regarding it ... accordingly they removed it, and put it in the chapter house.

Giorgio Vasari, *Lives of the Painters* (1568)

Don't be daft. You don't get any pornography on there, not on the telly. Get filth, that's all. The only place you get pornography is in yer Sunday papers.

Alf Garnett, in Johnny Speight's sitcom Till Death Us Do Part

I don't think pornography is very harmful, but it is terribly, terribly boring.

Noël Coward, quoted in the Observer, *24 September 1972*

A Doctor writes:

In the same way aspirin eases a headache, and penicillin battles the flu, a dose of pornography can work medicinal magic on sufferers of sexual stress.

Dr Jay Mann, in a Florida courtroom (1977)

Married **LOVE**

Courtship is to marriage as a witty prologue is to a very dull play.

William Congreve, *The Old Bachelor* (1693)

20-YEAR FRIENDSHIP ENDS AT ALTAR

Newspaper headline

Prostitutes for pleasure, concubines for service, wives for breeding.

Richard Burton, explorer

There are a lot of women who live with pot-bellied pigs.

Catherine Zeta-Jones

A man marries to have a home, but also because he doesn't want to be bothered with sex and all that sort of thing.

W. Somerset Maugham, The Circle *(1921)*

Wedlock: the deep, deep peace of the double bed after the hurly-burly of the chaise longue.

Mrs Patrick Campbell

Duke of Edinburgh: Do you think that sex ought to take place before the wedding?
Archbishop of Canterbury: No, not if it delays the ceremony.

Apocryphal tale

Conversation like television set on honeymoon – unnecessary.

Peter Sellers, as Mr Wang in Murder by Death *(1976)*

The majority of persons choose their wives with as little prudence as they eat. They see a trull with nothing else to recommend her but a pair of thighs and choice hunkers, and so smart to void their seed that they marry her at once. They imagine they can live in marvellous contentment with handsome feet and ambrosial buttocks. Most men are accredited fools shortly after they leave the womb.

Edward Dahlberg, The Carnal Myth *(1968)*

Marriage is the price men pay for sex, sex is the price women pay for marriage.

Anon.

Marriage is popular because it provides the maximum of temptation with the maximum of opportunity.

George Bernard Shaw, Maxims for Revolutionists *(1903)*

Getting married is very much like going to a restaurant with friends. You order what you want, then when you see what the other fellow has, you wish you had ordered that.

Anon.

MARRIAGE VS CELIBACY

As to marriage or celibacy, let a man take which covrse he will, he will be svre to repent.
Socrates

Marriage has many pains, but celibacy has no pleasures.
Samuel Johnson

They say a woman should be a cook in the kitchen and a whore in bed. Unfortunately, my wife is a whore in the kitchen and a cook in bed.

Anonymous man from Sunderland, quoted in Geoffrey Gorer,
Exploring English Character (1955)

Q: What's the difference between a new husband and new dog?
A: After a year the dog's still pleased to see you.

Anon.

And why do people wilfully exhaust their strength in promiscuous living, when their wives are on hand from bridal night until old age – to be taken when required, like fish from a private pond.

Ihara Saikaku, *The Japanese Family Storehouse* (1688)

Make love not war? I'm married, I do both.

Anon.

Constance: I'm tired of being the modern wife.
Martha: What do you mean by the modern wife?
Constance: A prostitute who doesn't deliver the goods.

W. Somerset Maugham, The Constant Wife *(1926)*

Personally I know nothing about sex because I have always been married.

Zsa Zsa Gabor

Zsa Zsa Gabor got married as a one-off and it was so successful she turned it into a series.

Bob Hope.

My mother said it was simple to keep a man – you must be a maid in the living room, a cook in the kitchen and a whore in the bedroom. I said I'd hire the other two and take care of the bedroom bit.

Jerry Hall, quoted in the Observer, *6 October 1985*

When my husband complained to me that he couldn't remember when we last had sex I said, 'Well I can, and that's why we ain't doing it.'

Roseanne Barr

A WORD ABOUT PORNOGRAPHY

You'll need it. Lots of it. The dirty, filthy, degrading kind. But keep it *well hidden*! Don't discount secret wall panels, trick drawers, holes in the yard, etc., especially if you have teenage boys or a Baptist wife with a housecleaning obsession. Also keep in mind that you could die at any moment, and nothing puts a crimp in a funeral worse than having the bereaved wonder what kind of sick, perverted beast you were under that kind and genteel exterior.

John Hughes, 'Very Married Sex', National Lampoon, 1979

The other night I said to my wife Ruth, 'Do you feel that the sex and excitement has gone out of our marriage?' Ruth said, 'I'll discuss it with you during the next commercial.'

Milton Berle

My wife is a sex object. Every time I ask for sex, she objects.

Les Dawson

Jefferson: I don't want to live with Marcy anymore. She wants sex all the time. I mean, sex with your pregnant wife is like putting gas in the tank of a car you already wrecked.
Al: Thank God my wife pulls into self-serve.

Lines from TV show Married … with Children

I've never yet met a man who could look after me. I don't need a husband. What I need is a wife.

Joan Collins, quoted in the Observer, *26 July 1987, after the end of her fourth (but by no means last) marriage*

After a quarrel, a husband says to his wife, 'You know, I was a fool when I married you.'
   She replies, 'Yes, dear, but I was in love and didn't notice.'

Anon.

I read recently that love is entirely a matter of chemistry. That must be why my wife treats me like toxic waste.

David Bissonette

Emily, I have a little confession to make. I really am a horse doctor. But marry me and I'll never look at any other horse.

Hackenbush to Mrs Upjohn in A Day at the Races *(1937)*

Before we make love my husband takes a pain killer.

Joan Rivers

Marriage is like a bank account. You put it in, you take it out, you lose interest.

Professor Irwin Corey

For their 25th wedding anniversary, they gave each other inscribed tombstones. Hers read 'Here lies my wife, cold as usual,' while his read 'Here lies my husband, stiff at last.'

Jack South

You may marry the man of your dreams, ladies, but fourteen years later you're married to a couch that burps.

Roseanne Barr

Real mothers think sex is like full-time employment – it's a nice idea, but it'll never happen again in their lifetime.

Victoria Wood

DOUBLE TROUBLE

Bigamy is having one wife too many.
Monogamy is the same.

Oscar Wilde, attributed

Spaulding: Are we going to get married?
Mrs Teasdale: But that's bigamy.
Spaulding: Yes, and it's bigame too.

Lines from Animal Crackers *(1930)*

There was an old man of Lyme
Who married three wives at a time.
When asked 'Why a third?'
He replied, 'One's absurd,
And bigamy, sir, is a crime.'

Anon.

Accursed from birth they be
Who seek to find monogamy,
Pursuing it from bed to bed –
I think they would be better dead.

Dorothy Parker, Reuben's Children *(1937)*

Dear wife, I acknowledge receipt of your complaint number 387,501.

W.C. Fields

Q: Why do married men gain weight while bachelors don't?
A: Bachelors go to the refrigerator, see nothing they want, then go to bed. Married guys go to the bed, see nothing they want, then go to the refrigerator.

Anon.

Getting married for sex is like buying a 747 for the free peanuts.

Jeff Foxworthy

Marriage is a great institution. But I'm not ready to be institutionalized yet.

Mae West

My husband and I had our best sex during our divorce. It was like cheating on our lawyers.

Priscilla Lopez, Cheaper to Keep Her

Alimony is the screwing you get for the screwing you got.

Graffito

Still At **IT** (Or Not)

Geriatric Sex

Just because there's snow on the roof, it doesn't mean the boiler has gone out.

Anon.

I'm a double bagger. Not only does my husband put a bag over my face when we're making love, but he also puts a bag over his head in case mine falls off.

Joan Rivers

Older women are best because they always think they may be doing it for the last time.

Ian Fleming

A man's only as old as the woman he feels.

Groucho Marx

I only take Viagra when I'm with more than one woman.

Jack Nicholson, quoted in the Observer, *8 February 2004*

Responding to suggestions of a liaison between herself and the 99-year-old Sir Richard Mayer, the 86-year-old Lady Diana Cooper commented:

My dear, when you are my age you will realize that what you need is the maturer man.

In my thirties I was doing it, in my forties I was organizing it and now, unfortunately, I can only talk about it.

Cynthia Paine, former madam, in the Guardian, *27 March 2004*

After 50 his [a man's] performance is of poor quality, the intervals between are wide, and its satisfactions of no great value to either party.

Mark Twain, Letters from the Earth *(1909)*

No. Not too old at fifty-three.
A worn defeated fool like me.
Still the tickling lust devours
Long stretches of my waking hours.
Busty girls in flowered scanties
Hitching down St Michael panties.
Easing off their wet-look boots
To step into their birthday suits.

Alan Bennett, Habeas Corpus *(1973)*

*Is it not strange that desire should so
many years outlive performance?*

William Shakespeare, *Henry IV, Part II* (1597)

*After thirty years I am old and without use:
Yours too wide, mine too weak.*

Yuan-wu

*John Anderson, my jo, John,
    When first that ye began,
Ye had as good a tail-tree,
    As ony ither man;
But now it's waxen wan, John,
    And wrinkles to and fro;
I've twa gae-ups for ae gae-down,
    John Anderson, my jo.*

Robert Burns (attributed), 'John Anderson, My Jo', from *The Merry Muses* (tail-tree = 'penis')

The three stages of a man's sex life: tri-weekly, try weekly and try weakly.

Anon.

I'm sixty-one today,
A year beyond the barrier,
And what was once a Magic Flute
Is now a Water Carrier.

Anon., referring to operas by Mozart and Cherubini

When you hit seventy you sleep sounder, you feel
more alive than when you were thirty. Obviously
it's healthier to have women on your mind than on
your knees.

Maurice Chevalier

Sex in your seventies is like waiting for the
plumber: you stay in all day and nobody comes.

John Mortimer

Sex at the age of eighty-four is a wonderful
experience. Especially the one in the winter.

Milton Berle

I have my eighty-seventh birthday coming up and
people ask what I'd most appreciate getting. I'll
tell you: a paternity suit.

George Burns

On seeing an attractive young woman, the 87-year-old Oliver
Wendell Holmes commented:

Oh to be seventy again!

> A 25-year-old Indian man has married his 80-year-old grandmother because he wanted to take care of her. 'I felt she needed extra care,' he said. 'I can look after her better as a husband than as a grandson.'
>
> *The* Guardian, *20 March 2004, reporting on a wedding in Panchpara, India*

Sex at age ninety is like trying to shoot pool with a rope.

George Burns

I'm at that age now where just putting my cigar in its holder is a thrill.

George Burns

An old man of ninety got married,
The bride was so young and so bold,
In his car they both went honeymooning –
She married the old man for gold.
A year later he was a daddy,
At ninety he still had the knack;
He took one look at the baby –
And then gave the chauffeur the sack.

Max Miller

Adultery

A Game for Adults

Do infants enjoy infancy as much as adults enjoy adultery?

Anon.

Merely innocent flirtation –
Not quite adultery, but adulteration.

Lord Byron, *Don Juan* (1824)

A sure sign that a man is going to be unfaithful is if he has a penis.

Jo Brand

Here's to our wives and sweethearts – may they never meet.

John Bunny

1. Never hunt south of the Thames.
2. Never drink port after champagne.
3. Never have your wife in the morning lest something better should turn up during the day.

Anon., quoted in Laurence Olivier, Confessions of an Actor *(1982)*

What's the three words you never want to hear while making love? 'Honey, I'm home.'

Ken Hammond

A couple are in bed when the phone rings.

'Who was it?' asks the man.

'My husband,' she says. 'But relax. He says he's down the pub with you.'

Anon.

Q: What is the one thing that all men at singles bars have in common ?

A: They're married.

Anon.

Do not adultery commit;
Advantage rarely comes of it.

Arthur Hugh Clough, 'The Latest Decalogue' (1862)

Adultery is the application of democracy to love.

H.L. Mencken, A Book of Burlesques (1920), 'Sententiæ'

One man's folly is often another man's wife.

Helen Rowland, Reflections of a Bachelor Girl (1903)

The Love Bird is 100 per cent faithful to his mate, as long as they are locked together in the same cage.

Will Cuppy

There are few who would not rather be taken in adultery than provincialism.

Aldous Huxley, Antic Hay *(1923)*

Wendle: I'm not a suspicious woman but I don't think my husband 'as been entirely faithful to me.
Pellet: Whatever makes you think that?
Wendle: My last child doesn't resemble him in the least.

Noël Coward, 'Law and Order', in This Year of Grace *(1928)*

I know many married men, I even know a few happily married men, but I don't know one who wouldn't fall down the first open coal-hole running after the first pretty girl who gave him a wink.

George Jean Nathan

A man comes home early and finds his wife in bed hard at it with another man.

'What on earth are you doing?' he shouts.

His wife turns to her lover and says, 'See, I told you he was thick as two short planks.'

Anon.

My wife only likes to have sex in places where there is a risk of getting caught. Well, I *have* caught her – numerous times, in fact.

Brad Osberg

Dates used to be made days or even weeks in advance. Now dates tend to be made the day after. That is, you get a phone call from someone who says, 'If anyone asks, I was out to dinner with you last night, okay?'

P.J. O'Rourke, Modern Manners *(1983)*

Moses comes down from the mountain after getting the ten commandments from God. At the bottom he sees the Children of Israel waiting. He says, 'Look. I've got some good news and some bad news. First the good news. There's only ten. And now the bad news. Adultery's in.'

Carol Clewlow, A Woman's Guide to Adultery *(1984)*

A hot-tempered girl of Caracas
Was wed to a samba-mad jackass.
When he started to cheat her
With a dark señorita
She kicked him right in the maracas.

Anon.

I said to the wife, 'Guess what I heard in the pub? They reckon the milkman has made to love to every woman in this road except one.' And she said, 'I'll bet it's that stuck-up Phyllis at number 23.'

Max Kauffman

I'm married, but I don't wear a wedding ring because I've found that it tends to give women the impression that I'm unavailable.

Bill Muse

Asked how many husbands she'd had:

You mean apart from my own?

Zsa Zsa Gabor

'Come, Come' said Tom's father 'at your time of life,
There's no longer excuse for this playing the rake –
It is time you should think, boy, of taking a wife' –
'Why so it is, father – whose wife shall I take?'

Anon., 'A Joke Versified' (19th century)

**I say I don't sleep with married men,
but what I mean is that I don't sleep
with happily married men.**

Britt Ekland

When a man steals your wife, there is no better revenge than to let him keep her.

Sacha Guitry

There is one thing I would break up over, and that is if she caught me with another woman. I won't stand for that.

Steve Martin

My wife has cut our lovemaking down to once a month, but I know two guys she's cut out entirely.

Rodney Dangerfield

I told my wife the truth. I told her I was seeing a psychiatrist. Then she told me the truth: that she was seeing a psychiatrist, two plumbers and a bartender.

Rodney Dangerfield

Asked whether he had ever smoked a spliff in the 1960s:

Only when committing adultery.

Senator Wyche Fowler

There were three of us in this marriage.

Diana, Princess of Wales, referring to Prince Charles's long-running liaison with Camilla Parker-Bowles in an interview on BBC TV's Panorama, *20 November 1995*

THE WOMAN AND THE MAN GUILTY OF FORNICATION . . .
FLOG EACH OF THEM WITH A HUNDRED LASHES.
THE KORAN. STONING SEEMS TO BE MORE THE THING
THESE DAYS.

IF A MAN BE FOUND LYING WITH A WOMAN MARRIED TO
A HUSBAND, THEN THEY SHALL BOTH OF THEM DIE.
DEUTERONOMY 22:22

In the light of this, the following may be an example of
wishful thinking:

I have looked on a lot of women with lust. I've
committed adultery in my heart many times.
God recognizes I will do this and forgives me.

Jimmy Carter, interview in Playboy, *November 1976*

Apparently Mr Carter was mistaken:

Adultery in your heart is committed not only
when you look with excessive sexual desire at
a woman who is not your wife, but also if you
look in the same manner at your wife.

Pope John Paul II

Thou shalt not commit adultery ... unless in the mood.

W.C. Fields

A Code of Honour: never approach a friend's girlfriend or wife with mischief as your goal ... Unless she's *really* attractive.

Bruce Jay Friedman, 'Sex and the Lonely Guy', in Esquire, *1977*

Like the ski resort full of girls looking for husbands and husbands looking for girls, the situation is not as symmetrical as it might seem.

Alan McKay

Reading someone else's newspaper is like sleeping with someone else's wife. Nothing seems to be precisely in the right place, and when you find what you are looking for, it is not clear then how to respond to it.

Malcolm Bradbury, Stepping Westward *(1975)*

You know, of course, that the Tasmanians, who never committed adultery, are now extinct.

W. Somerset Maugham, 'The Bread-Winner' (1930)

I've been in love with the same woman for 41 years. If my wife finds out she'll kill me.

Henny Youngman

COVETING THY NEIGHBOUR'S UDDERS: SAGACITY FROM THE CLASSICS

THE GRASS IS ALWAYS GREENER, AND . . .
THE NEIGHBOVR'S HERD HAS RICHER VDDERS.
OVID, THE ART OF LOVE (1ST CENTURY AD)

It's those Latin types who are always at it …

What men call gallantry, and gods adultery,
Is much more common where the climate's sultry.

Lord Byron, *Don Juan* (1819–24), I, 63

The Latin is quite urbane in these matters. Thus an 18th-century Frenchman to his wife, whom he had caught *in flagrante delicto*:

Madame, you should be more careful. What if someone other than I had come across you thus?

Duc de Richelieu

Even the English can be infected with this worldliness:

A mistress should be like a little country retreat near the town, not to dwell in constantly, but only for a night and away.

William Wycherley, The Country Wife, *I (1675); Dorilant speaking*

As I grow older and older,
And totter towards the tomb,
I find that I care less and less
Who goes to bed with whom.

Dorothy L. Sayers, 'That's Why I Never Read Modern Novels'

On his marriage to Joanne Woodward:

Why fool around with hamburger when you can have steak at home?

Paul Newman

Tales of adultery are much improved by period costumes.

Mason Cooley, City Aphorisms, Sixth Selection *(1989)*

My debaucheries do not trouble my husband one jot … he is no more bothered by my cavortings than I would be by his. I could fuck the whole world without giving him the slightest pain.

Madame de Saint-Ange, in Marquis de Sade, Philosophy of the Boudoir *(1795)*

Being a **MAN**

Like Being Shackled to a Maniac

SOMEONE ASKED SOPHOCLES, 'HOW DO YOU FEEL NOW
ABOUT SEX? ARE YOU STILL ABLE TO HAVE A WOMAN?'
HE REPLIED, 'HVSH, MAN; MOST GLADLY INDEED I AM
RID OF IT ALL, AS THOVGH I HAD ESCAPED FROM A
MAD AND STRANGE MASTER.'

PLATO, REPUBLIC

Q: What do you call a man with 99 per cent of his
brain missing?
A: Castrated.

Anon.

Never let the little head do the thinking for the
big head.

Advice to teenage boys, quoted in Friendly Advice *compiled by Jon
Winokur*

Q: Why do men have pet names for their penises?
A: Because they don't like to take orders from a
stranger.

Anon.

A standing prick hath no conscience.

Proverbial saying

Q: How can you tell that God is a woman?
A: If God were a man, he would have put the balls on the inside.

Anon.

Girls are always running through my mind. They don't dare walk.

Andy Gibb

A student undergoing a word-association test was asked why a snowstorm put him in mind of sex. He replied frankly: 'Because everything does.'

Honor Tracy

A man who is old enough to know better is always on the look out for a girl who isn't.

Anon.

Men are those creatures with two legs and eight hands.

Jayne Mansfield

Hacking is like sex. You get in, you get out, and hope that you didn't leave something behind that can be traced back to you.

Anon.

What most men desire is a virgin who is also a whore.

Edward Dahlberg, Reasons of the Heart *(1965), 'On Lust'*

Outside every thin woman is a fat man trying to get in.

Katherine Whitehorn

If the devil were to offer me a resurgence of what is commonly called virility, I'd decline. 'Just keep my liver and lungs in good working order,' I'd reply, 'so I can go on drinking and smoking!'

Luis Buñuel, My Last Sigh *(1983)*

Q: Why do men snore when they lie on their backs?
A: Because their balls fall over their ass-hole and they vapour-lock.

Anon.

Gay **KNIGHTS**

Asked by US immigration officials whether he was a practising homosexual:

Certainly not. I'm absolutely perfect.

Quentin Crisp

I'm not really a homosexual. I just help them out when they're busy.

Frank Carson

Q: Why is it so hard for women to find men who are sensitive and caring?
A: Because those men already have boyfriends.

Anon.

My hope is that gays will be running the world, because then there would be no more war. Just a greater emphasis on military apparel.

Roseanne Barr

We had gay burglars the other night. They broke in and rearranged the furniture.

Robin Williams

A tired old fairy from Rome
Took a leprechaun back to his home.
As he entered the elf
He said to himself
I'd be much better off in a gnome.

Anon.

There are three kinds of pianists: Jewish pianists, homosexual pianists, and bad pianists.

Vladimir Horowitz

WHAT THE GOOD BOOK SAYS 8

IF A MAN ALSO LIE WITH MANKIND, AS HE LIETH WITH A WOMAN, BOTH OF THEM HAVE COMMITTED AN ABOMINATION: THEY SHALL SURELY BE PUT TO DEATH; THEIR BLOOD SHALL BE UPON THEM.
LEVITICUS 20:13

The authors of Leviticus proscribe homosexuality – and so do all good Christians. But Leviticus also proscribes rare meat, bacon, shellfish, and the wearing of nylon mixed with wool. If Leviticus were to be obeyed in every instance, the garment trade would collapse.

Gore Vidal, Pink Triangle and Yellow Star *(1979)*

It was out of the closet and into the streets for the nation's homosexuals in the 1970s. This didn't do much for the streets but, on the other hand, your average closet has improved immeasurably.

John Weidman and Rick Meyerowitz, in National Lampoon, *1980*

I became one of the stately homos of England.

Quentin Crisp, The Naked Civil Servant *(1968)*

It's better to be black than gay because when you're black you don't have to tell your mother.

Charles Pierce

Admittedly, a homosexual can be conditioned to react sexually to a woman, or to an old boot for that matter. In fact, both homo- and heterosexual experimental subjects *have* been conditioned to react sexually to an old boot, and you can save a lot of money that way.

William Burroughs, The Adding Machine *(1985), 'Civilian Defense'*

My mother made me a homosexual.
If I bought her the wool, would she make me one too?

Graffito, in two different hands

The Air Force pinned a medal on me for killing a man and discharged me for making love to one.

Leonard Matlovich, formerly of the US Air Force, in 1975

Just because you're gay doesn't mean you go to orgies.

Rabbi Lionel Blue, quoted in the Observer, *8 February 2004*

If Michelangelo had been straight, the Sistine Chapel would have been wallpapered.

Robin Tyler, speech at a gay-rights rally, 1988

There's this illusion that homosexuals have sex and heterosexuals fall in love. That's completely untrue. Everybody wants to be loved.

Boy George

There was a young Fellow of Wadham
Who asked for a ticket to Sodom.
When they said, 'We prefer
Not to issue them, sir,'
He said, 'Don't call me sir, call me modom.'

Anon.

I have heard some say … [homosexual] practices
are allowed in France and in other NATO
countries. We are not French, and we are not
other nationals. We are British, thank God!

*Lord Montgomery of Alamein, speaking in the House of Lords, 24
May 1965, on the second reading of the Sexual Offences Bill*

The only queer people are those who don't love
anybody.

Rita Mae Brown, speech, 28 August 1982

Homosexuals, like Jews, often find themselves
numbered among their enemies' best friends.

Frederic Raphael

Should everyone found guilty of Oscar Wilde's crime
be imprisoned, there would be a very surprising
emigration from Eton, Rugby, Harrow and
Winchester to the jails of Pentonville and Holloway.

W.T. Stead, Review of Reviews (1895)

For men who want to flee Family Man America and never come back, there is a guaranteed solution: homosexuality is the new French Foreign Legion.

Florence King, Reflections in a Jaundiced Eye, 'From Captain Marvel to Captain Valium' (1989)

One of my ministers found half-naked with a guardsman in Hyde Park? Last Wednesday? The coldest night of the year? Makes you proud to be British.

Winston Churchill, allegedly

A lot of gay people who are not dealing with their homosexuality get into right-wing politics.

Armistead Maupin, quoted in the Guardian, *22 April 1988*

There was a young Fellow of King's
Who cared not for whores and such things:
His height of desire
Was a boy in the choir
With a bum like a jelly on springs.

Anon.

Girl-on-Girl
STUFF

Were kisses all the joys in bed,
One woman would another wed.
William Shakespeare, *Sonnets to Sundry Notes of Music*, IV

Asked whether she was a lesbian by a male heckler:

Are you my alternative?

Florynce Kennedy

Some of us are becoming the men we wanted to marry.

Gloria Steinem

I chased a girl for two years only to discover that her tastes were exactly like mine: We were both crazy about girls.

Groucho Marx

On being told that he couldn't film Lillian Hellman's play *The Children's Hour* because it involved lesbians:

OK, so we make them Albanians.

Samuel Goldwyn

*My breasts, if it is not too bold a figure to call so two
hard, firm, rising hillocks, that just began to shew
themselves, or signify anything to the touch, employ'd and
amus'd her hands a-while, till, slipping down lower, over
a smooth track, she could just feel the soft silky down that
had but a few months before put forth and garnish'd the
mount-pleasant of those parts, and promised to spread a
grateful shelter over the seat of the most exquisite
sensation, and which had been, till that instant, the seat of
the most insensible innocence. Her fingers play'd and
strove to twine in the young tendrils of that moss, which
nature has contrived at once for use and ornament.
But, not contented with these outer posts, she now attempts
the main spot, and began to twitch, to insinuate, and at
length to force an introduction of a finger into the quick
itself, in such a manner, that had she not proceeded by
insensible gradations that inflamed me beyond the power
of modesty to oppose its resistance to their progress, I
should have jump'd out of bed and cried for help against
such strange assaults.*

John Cleland, *Memoirs of a Lady of Pleasure*, better known as
Fanny Hill (1748–9)

Like most men, I am consumed with desire
whenever a lesbian gets within twenty feet.
Taki

Ye Olde Red-Hotte Lesbo Action

Then on your back lie down upon the bed,
And lift your petticoats above your head;
I'll shew you a new piece of lechery,
For I'll be the man, you shall the woman be.
Your thin transparent smock, my dear remove
That last bless'd cover to the scene of love.
What's this I see, you fill me with surprise,
Your charming beauties dazzle quite my eyes!
Gods! what a leg is here! what lovely thighs!
A belly too, as polish'd iv'ry white,
And then a cunt would charm an anchorite!
Oh! now I wish I were a man indeed,
That I might gain thy pretty maidenhead,
But since, my dear, I can't my wish obtain,
Let's now proceed t'instruct you in the game;
That game that brings the most substantial bliss;
For swiving of all games the sweetest is.
Ope wide your legs, and throw them round by back,
And clasp your snowy arms about my neck.
Your buttocks then move nimbly up and down.
Whilst with my hand I thrust the dildo home.
You'll feel the titulation by and by;

> *Have you no pleasure yet, no tickling joy?*
> *Oh! yes, yes, now I faint, I die.*
> Johannes Meursius *The Delights of Venus*
> (17th century)

My lesbianism is an act of Christian charity. All those women out there are praying for a man, and I'm giving them my share.
Rita Mae Brown, in 1978

Somewhere she had once heard that women – lesbians – were experts at this because they knew what another woman wanted. That wasn't true. When she and Victoria had done it, it had been like trying out some strange Japanese cuisine, something that wriggled, still alive, in a dish. Or having to swallow the contents of a bearded mussel attached to a rock, while all the while one knew the tide was rapidly coming in.
Tama Janowitz, Peyton Amberg *(2003)*

To Graham Norton:

Just to annoy the *Daily Mail*, shall you and I get married?
Sandi Toksvig

A pansy who lived in Khartoum
Took a lesbian up to his room.
And they argued a lot
About who should do what
And how and with which and to whom.

Anon.

If we accept the notion ... that AIDS represents
God's punishment to erring homosexuals, then it
stands to reason that lesbians – virtually
untouched by AIDS or sexually transmitted
diseases – must be God's chosen people.

Letter to Newsweek *(1980s)*

AC/**DC**

Swinging Both Ways

Bisexuality immediately doubles your chances for a date on a Saturday night.

Woody Allen, quoted in The New York Times, *1 December 1975*

I'm glad I'm not bisexual. I couldn't stand being rejected by men as well as women.

Bernard Manning

On being asked whether his first sexual experience was with a boy or a girl:

I was far too polite to ask.

Gore Vidal

Honestly, I like everything. Boyish girls, girlish boys, the thick, the thin. Which is a problem when I'm walking down the street.

Angelina Jolie

I'm a sex machine to both genders. It's all very exhausting. I need a lot of sleep.

Rupert Everett

If you're feeling randy
And a girl or boy is handy
Don't mope for it,
Just grope for it!

Horace, *Satires* (1st century BC) (loosely translated)

Nor shall our love-fits, Chloris be forgot,
When each the well-looked linkboy strove t'enjoy,
And the best kiss was the deciding lot
Whether the boy fucked you, or I the boy.

John Wilmot, Earl of Rochester, *'The Disabled Debaucher'*
(17th century)

I could have loved boys, but I prefer girls. If she
bores me as a girl, I can use her like a boy.

J.W. von Goethe, *Venetian Epigrams* (c.1786)

I am the kind of bisexual who sleeps only with men.

Todd Haynes, US film maker, interview in the Guardian, *13 April 1996*

I am a bisexual … I suppose it's the best thing that
ever happened to me. Fun, too.

David Bowie, interview, February 1976

Boys Will Be
GIRLS

Transvestites and
Transsexuals

I saw on television the other day some men who like to dress up as women and when they do they can no longer parallel park.

Roseanne Barr

I'm an action transvestite really, so it's running, jumping, climbing trees … putting on make-up when you're up there …

Eddie Izzard

I'm not actually half girl/half boy. I've worked this out. I'm sort of all boy, plus extra girl.

Eddie Izzard, quoted in the Observer, *30 November 2003*

Queens, unlike feminists, know that woman is the dominatrix of the universe.

Camille Paglia, Vamps and Tramps *(1994)*

Boy George is all England needs – another queen who can't dress.

Joan Rivers

I wish I could change my sex as I change my shirt.

André Breton

Said a butcher's apprentice from Frome
Who aspired to be bride and not groom,
'With some knives from the shop
I'll perform my own op.'
And these words are inscribed on his tomb.

Anon.

Actually, I really want to play Princess Leia.
Stick some big pastries on my head.
Now, that would be interesting.

Ewan McGregor, on acting in Star Wars

The Battle of the
SEXES

Men vs Women

Women are like fine wine. They all start out fresh, fruity and intoxicating to the mind and then turn full-bodied with age until they go all sour and vinegary and give you a headache.

Anon.

It's true that all men are pigs. The trick is to tame one who knows how to find truffles.

Lev L. Spiro

> **Q. What do you call the useless piece of flesh at the end of a penis?**
> **A. A man.**
>
> *Anon.*

Q: What's the difference between a bar and a clitoris ?

A: Most men have no trouble finding a bar.

Anon.

Word to the wise: women want men with flat stomachs and fat wallets. My sex life still hasn't recovered from getting it backwards.

Derek Cockram

Men reach their sexual peak at eighteen. Women reach theirs at thirty-five. Do you get the feeling that God is playing a practical joke?

Rita Rudner

Women want a lot of things from one man. Conversely, men want one thing from a lot of women.

Anon.

Women complain about sex more often than men. Their gripes fall into two categories: (1) Not enough. (2) Too much.

Ann Landers, Ann Landers Says Truth is Stranger … *(1968)*

Men get laid, but women get screwed.

Quentin Crisp

My understanding of women only goes as far as the pleasures. When it comes to the pain, I'm like every other bloke. I don't want to know.

Michael Caine as Alfie, in Alfie *(1966), screenplay by Bill Naughton*

Men talk to women so they can sleep with them and women sleep with men so they can talk to them.

Jay McInerney, Brightness Falls *(1992)*

One half of the world cannot understand the pleasures of the other.

Jane Austen, *Emma* (1816)

How do you know if it's time to wash the dishes and clean your house? Look inside your pants. If you find a penis in there, it's not time.

Jo Brand

Seems to me the basic conflict between men and women, sexually, is that men are like firemen. To men, sex is an emergency, and no matter what we're doing we can be ready in two minutes. Women, on the other hand, are like fire. They're very excited, but the conditions have to be exactly right for it to occur.

Jerry Seinfeld

There is, of course, no reason for the existence of the male sex except that sometimes one needs help with moving the piano.

Rebecca West

IF MEN WROTE FOR *COSMOPOLITAN*

Q: My husband wants to experience three-in-a-bed-sex with me and my sister.

A: Your husband is clearly devoted to you. He cannot get enough of you, so he goes for the next best thing: your sister. Far from being an issue, this will bring all of your family closer together. Why not get some cousins involved? If you are still apprehensive, then let him go with your relatives, buy him a nice, expensive present, and cook him a nice meal and don't mention this aspect of his behaviour.

Q: My husband continually asks me to perform oral sex with him.

A: Do it. Sperm is not only great tasting, but has only 10 calories a spoonful. It is nutritious and helps you to keep your figure and gives a great glow to the skin. Interestingly, a man knows this. His offer to you to perform oral sex with him is totally selfless. Oral sex is extremely painful for a man. This shows he loves you. Best thing to do is thank him, buy him a nice, expensive present, and cook him a nice meal.

Q: My husband has too many nights out with the boys.

A: This is perfectly natural behaviour and it should be encouraged. The man is a hunter and he needs to prove his prowess with other men. Far from being pleasurable, a night out with the boys is a stressful affair, and to get back to you is a relief for your partner. Just look back at how emotional and happy the man is when he returns to his stable home. Best thing to do is to buy him an expensive present, and cook him a nice meal, and don't mention this aspect of his behaviour.

Q: My husband is uninterested in foreplay.

A: Foreplay to a man is very hurtful. What it means is that you do not love your man as much as you should – he has to do a lot of work to get you in the mood. Abandon all wishes in this area, and make it up to him by buying a nice, expensive present, and cooking him a nice meal.

Q: My husband never gives me an orgasm.

A: The female orgasm is a myth. It is fostered by militant, man-hating feminists and is a danger to the family unit. Don't mention it again to him and show your love to him by buying a nice, expensive present and don't forget to cook him a delicious meal.

Q: How do I know if I'm ready for sex?
A: Ask your boyfriend. He will know when the time is right. When it comes to love and sex, men are much more responsible, since they're not as confused emotionally as women. It's a proven fact.

Q: Should I have sex on the first date?
A: YES. Before, if possible.

Q: Does the size of the penis matter?
A: Yes. Although many women believe that quality, not quantity, is important, studies show this is simply not true. The average erect male penis measures about three inches. Anything longer than that is extremely rare and, if by some chance your lover's sexual organ is four inches or over, you should go down on your knees and thank your lucky stars and do everything possible to please him, such as doing his laundry, cleaning his apartment and buying him an expensive gift.

While redecorating, I realized my wife and I have drastically different tastes in furniture. She wanted to keep only the pieces that reflected the French provincial theme she was creating; I wanted to keep all the stuff we'd had sex on.

Brad Osberg

Women need a reason to have sex. Men just need a place.

Billy Crystal

Women might be able to fake orgasms. But men can fake a whole relationship.

Sharon Stone

The more I see of men, the less I like them. If I could but say so of women too, all would be well.

Lord Byron, Journal, 1814

Ah, yes, divorce, from the Latin word meaning to rip out a man's genitals through his wallet.

Robin Williams

A woman tries to get all she can out of a man, and a man tries to get all he can into a woman.

Isaac Goldberg

The difference between snowmen and snow-women is snowballs.

Anon.

According to a new survey, women say they feel more comfortable undressing in front of men than they do undressing in front of other women. They say that women are too judgmental, where, of course, men are just grateful.

Robert De Niro

How to impress a woman?
Compliment her, cuddle her, kiss her, caress her, love her, stroke her, tease her, comfort her, protect her, hug her, hold her, spend money on her, wine and dine her, buy things for her, listen to her, care for her, stand by her, support her, buy flowers for her, go to the ends of the earth for her ...

How to impress a man?
Show up naked. Bring beer.

Anon.

This Sporting
LIFE

A little love-in before the main event can do you more good than a rub-down with *The Sporting Life*.

John Conteh, boxer

Being with a woman all night never hurt no professional baseball player. It's the staying up all night looking for one that does him in.

Charles 'Casey' Stengel, baseball coach

If you're going to get pissed or poke a girl, do it before midnight.

Mike Gatting, advice to his team as Middlesex captain in 1983

No one who knows jockeys could imagine them saying, 'Not tonight, darling, I am riding in the National tomorrow.'

Jenny Pitman, racehorse trainer

I think it's a great idea to talk during sex, as long as it's about snooker.

Steve 'Interesting' Davis, snooker player

I'm like the most expensive, exotic item on a gourmet menu. People can wonder about the sensuous delights of the dish, but they can't afford such an expensive luxury.

Anna Kournikova

Cricket is like sex films – they relieve frustration and tension.

Linda Lovelace, star of Deep Throat, *visits Lord's in 1974*

Controversial Wests Tigers winger John Hopoate has been suspended for 12 weeks after being found guilty by the NRL Judiciary of poking his fingers up the anuses of three North Queensland players. Accused of one of the most bizarre charges in the history of rugby league, or sport in general for that matter of fact, Hopoate was officially found guilty of 'unsportsmanlike interference'.

Sportal League

Football is a fertility festival. Eleven sperm trying to get into one egg. I feel sorry for the poor goalkeeper.

Björk, in 1995

Everyone knows which comes first when it's a question of cricket or sex.

Harold Pinter [It's cricket, stupid. Ed.]

Cricket-playing nations are capable of only limited amounts of sexual activity.

Letter published in the Bangkok Post, *1991*

If you'd given me the choice of beating four men and smashing in a goal from 30 yards against Liverpool or going to bed with Miss World, it would have been a difficult choice. Luckily I had both. It's just that you do one of those things in front of 50,000 people.

George Best

TIGER WOODS PLAYS WITH HIS OWN BALLS, NIKE SAYS

Newspaper headline

Both are very hard to go without, but I don't think sex could ever be as rewarding as winning the World Cup. It's not that sex is not great; just that the World Cup is every four years and sex is a lot more regular than that.

Ronaldo speaks after scoring twice to win the 2002 World Cup for Brazil against Germany, 30 June 2002

... the breakdown of his [Frank Worthington's] move to Liverpool in 1972 is one of the game's enduring urban legends. Having all but signed, the deal fell through because he failed a medical. The rumour was that he had a dose of the clap. In fact he had high blood pressure ... brought on by excessive sexual activity.

The Observer Sport Monthly, *on Frank Worthington, 4 November, 2001. Worthington's idiosyncratic biography was entitled* One Hump or Two?

When you swap shirts at the end of the match you expect it to smell bad. But Becks' smelt really nice.

Ronaldo. Hmmm.

The programme implied that ... he made love like he played cricket: slowly, methodically, but with the very real possibility that he might stay in all day.

Martin Kelner in the Guardian, *8 September 2003, describes the Channel 4 documentary* The Real Geoffrey Boycott, *on the famously slow-scoring Yorkshire batsman*

Mine's Bigger Than **YOURS**

Politicians

It would take the seriousness out of things like the Bay of Pigs or the Cuban Missile Crisis if you could just imagine JFK behind the bathroom door whacking it to Miss July once in a while.

Lenny Bruce

Fighting for peace is like fucking for virginity.

Graffito

A Serious Person writes:

Sex without class-consciousness cannot give satisfaction even if it is repeated until infinity.

Aldo Brandirali, Italian Marxist, in 1973

Alan Clark is not 65 going on 16. He is 65 going on 12.

Jane Clark

No wonder that girl was licking David Mellor's toes. She was probably trying to get as far away from his face as possible.

Tommy Docherty

Once we acknowledge everyone's a wanker … suddenly all authority figures disappear. You've got a bank manager, right, won't give you a ten quid overdraft. Look him in the eye – you're a wanker, aren't you? All world leaders – Gorbachev – wanker; Pope – wanker; even Mrs Thatch must occasionally slip the claw under the elastic.

Ben Elton

38A SUNDAY, DECEMBER 12, 1999
INTERNATIONAL
Clinton's firmness got results
TALKS

Clinton lied. A man might forget where he parks or where he lives, but he never forgets oral sex, no matter how bad it is.

Barbara Bush (apparently)

Still on Clinton:

A man will occasionally step on his dick, but he shouldn't stand on it.

Kris Kristofferson

I'm for a high-libido president! I applaud him if he gets up and picks up women.

Camille Paglia, Vamps and Tramps *(1994)*

CLINTON APOLOGIZES TO SYPHILIS VICTIMS

Newspaper headline

Monica Lewinsky went into a dry cleaners where a hard-of-hearing clerk had his back to her.

'I need to have this dress dry-cleaned.'

'Come again?'

'No, mustard.'

Anon.

I voted Republican this year; the Democrats left a bad taste in my mouth.

Monica Lewinsky [Believe it if you will. Ed.]

Political (In)Correctness

Then I said to her, 'So you're a feminist – how cute.'
Robin Williams

I'm not a breast man, I'm a breast person.
Anon.

'You old scrubber' came back as 'You ex-cleaning woman, you.'
Jilly Cooper, quoted in the Observer, *5 March 1995*

From the Woman's PC Phrasebook:
He *does not* undress you with his eyes. He has rather an IPM (Introspective Pornographic Moment).
Anon.

Sexual harassment at work – is it a problem for the self-employed?
Victoria Wood

If you keep the sexual harassment complaint forms in the bottom drawer, then you'll get a great view of the women's butts when they get one out.
Anon.

Come Sing Me a **SONG**

Sex and Music

Come sing me a bawdy song, and make me merry.

William Shakespeare, Henry IV, Part One, *III.iii; Falstaff speaking*

Give me some music – music, moody food
Of us that trade in love.

William Shakespeare, Antony and Cleopatra, *II.v; Cleopatra speaking*

Music and women I cannot but give way to, whatever my business is.

Samuel Pepys, Diary, 1666

The harpsichord:

Sounds like two skeletons copulating on a tin roof.

Sir Thomas Beecham

I conclude that musical notes and rhythms were first acquired by the male or female progenitors of mankind for the sake of charming the opposite sex.

Charles Darwin, The Descent of Man *(1871)*

Of Fauré's *Romances sans paroles*:

The sort of music a pederast might hum while raping a choirboy.

Marcel Proust, quoted in Musical Quarterly, *1924*

An Old Fusspot writes:

It might not be a bad idea for some teenagers, when they are being 'sent' by a piece of jazz, to ask themselves where the music stopped and the sex began and vice versa.

Beverley Nichols, in the 1960s

Music helps set a romantic mood. Some men believe that the only good music is live music. Imagine her surprise when you say, 'I don't need a stereo – I have an accordion!' Then imagine the sound of a door slamming.

Martin Mull

America

Yanking Yanks

Q: What's the definition of a Yankee?
A: Same thing as a quickie only you do it yourself.
Anon.

**Sex. In America an obsession.
In other parts of the world a fact.**

Marlene Dietrich, Marlene Dietrich's ABC, 'Sex' *(1962)*

That our popular art forms have become so
obsessed with sex has turned the USA into a
nation of hobbledehoys; as if grown people don't
have more vital concerns, such as taxes, inflation,
dirty politics, earning a living, getting an
education, or keeping out of jail.

Anita Loos, Kiss Hollywood Goodbye *(1974)*

France

Frolicking Frogs

To a Frenchman sex provides the most economical way to have fun.

Anita Loos, Kiss Hollywood Goodbye *(1974)*

A Vision in Pink somewhat surprisingly writes:

France is the only place where you can make love in the afternoon without people hammering on your door.

Barbara Cartland, in 1984

Weep not for little Leonie,
Abducted by a French Marquis!
Though loss of honour was a wrench,
Just think how it's improved her French.

Harry Graham, 'Compensation'

A delectable gal from Augusta
vowed that nobody ever had bussed her.
But an expert from France
took a bilingual chance
and the mixture of tongues quite nonplussed her.

Conrad Aiken, A Seizure of Limericks *(1965)*

No Sex Please, We're **BRITISH**

Continental people have a sex life; the English have hot-water bottles.

George Mikes, How to Be an Alien *(1946)*

The Englishman can get along with sex quite perfectly so long as he can pretend that it isn't sex but something else.

James Agate, 'Ego 1', 14 October 1932

The cold of the polar regions was nothing to the chill of an English bedroom.

Fridtjof Nansen, Norwegian explorer, quoted in Daniele Varè, The Laughing Diplomat *(1939)*

I did a picture in England one winter and it was so cold I almost got married.

Shelley Winters, quoted in The New York Times, *29 April 1956*

Most Englishmen can never get over the embarrassing fact that they were born in bed with a woman.

Anon. Scotsman

Picture Credits

The publishers would like to thank the following individuals and institutions for permission to reproduce the pictures on the pages listed below. Every effort has been made to trace the copyright holders. Weidenfeld & Nicolson apologise for any unintentional omissions and, if informed of such cases, shall make corrections in any future edition.

Page 8   www.humorandjokes.com
Page 21   www.bridgeman.co.uk / Chetham's
                Library, Manchester
Page 28-9   Corbis / Hulton-Deutsch Collection
Page 42   www.rudefun.com
Page 44   www.bridgeman.co.uk / City of
                Westminster Archive Centre (*The
                Covent Garden Night Mare*)
Page 53   www.rudefun.com
Page 61   www.rudefun.com
Page 66   www.humorandjokes.com
Page 71   www.rudefun.com
Page 73   Mary Evans Picture Library (*The Bald
                Prima Donna*)
Page 77   www.humorandjokes.com
Page 79   www.humorandjokes.com